PRAISE FOR *TRIN*

"In *Trinitarian Formation,* Chase Davis has made a substantial
contribution to the church's work in 'spiritual formation,'
which helps believers to grow toward Christian maturity,
sanctification in Christ. I'm delighted that he has made use of
my 'tri-perspectivalism' and that he has gone so deeply into it,
comparing it to the work of others I deeply respect, like James
K. A. Smith. This leads him into some fairly difficult concep-
tual areas. But he has analyzed these well and has formulated
them with clear, appropriate, and fetching illustrations. So this
volume speaks both to professional scholars and to church
workers. I hope this book gets a very wide distribution, and I
pray that God will use it to the edification of his people."

—JOHN M. FRAME, PROFESSOR OF SYSTEMATIC THEOLOGY AND
PHILOSOPHY EMERITUS, REFORMED THEOLOGICAL SEMINARY

"I have been told that great understanding can be found at
the crossroads of two seemingly unrelated fields. Chase's
book affirms this, for he demonstrates the power of applying
Frame's epistemological triad to James K. A. Smith's work on
discipleship. I recommend this book both as a way of seeing
how Frame's triad can be usefully applied, and also a means
of comprehensively recognizing where Smith's discipleship
model is helpful and where it can be improved."

—TIM MILLER, ASSISTANT PROFESSOR OF SYSTEMATIC THEOLOGY
AND APOLOGETICS, DETROIT BAPTIST THEOLOGICAL SEMINARY

"The ever-fertile, provocative 'Framean Triad' is standing the test of time. Wonderful to see theologian John Frame's motif tapped yet again, in this book for normative guidance in designing Christian spiritual formation, especially for thoughtful, devoted youth ministers. An important endeavor all round."

—ESTHER LIGHTCAP MEEK, AUTHOR OF *LOVING TO KNOW: INTRODUCING COVENANT EPISTEMOLOGY*

"A discipleship plan is crucial for pastoral success. After an analytical critique of prevailing discipleship models, in his book *Trinitarian Formation*, Chase Davis draws up the blueprints for just such a plan. Chase clearly demonstrates how Dr. John Frame's model of tri-perspectivalism is an effective model for every Christian's spiritual growth. Davis's analysis is a gift to every pastor, an invitation to think through and implement an effective model for making disciples ready to live out the Great Commission."

—DOUG LOGAN JR., PRESIDENT, GRIMKÉ SEMINARY, AND ASSOCIATE DIRECTOR, ACTS 29 GLOBAL NETWORK

"In this insightful work, Davis helps us think more deeply about the formation of Christian disciples. Not content to accept ready-made formulas for spiritual formation, he engages us in thoughtful reflection, drawing upon contemporary Christian thinkers and calling us to give greater thought to the task of making fully devoted followers of Jesus."

—DAVID M. GUSTAFSON, AUTHOR OF *MISSIONAL DISCIPLE-MAKING: DISCIPLE-MAKING FOR THE PURPOSE OF MISSION*

TRINITARIAN
FORMATION

TRINITARIAN FORMATION

A Theology of Discipleship in Light of the Father, Son, and Holy Spirit

J. CHASE DAVIS

foreword by Don J. Payne

WIPF & STOCK · Eugene, Oregon

TRINITARIAN FORMATION
A Theology of Discipleship in Light of the Father, Son, and Holy Spirit

Wipf & Stock
An Imprint of Wipf and Stock Publishers
199 W. 8th Ave., Suite 3
Eugene, OR 97401

www.wipfandstock.com

PAPERBACK ISBN: 978-1-7252-6159-4
HARDCOVER ISBN: 978-1-7252-6158-7
EBOOK ISBN: 978-1-7252-6160-0

01/12/21

This book is dedicated to Knox and Owen,
my sons who teach me daily
about formation and discipleship.

Contents

Foreword

STUDIES IN THEOLOGICAL METHOD easily remain sequestered in esoteric conversations that make sense only in theological laboratories. Make no mistake; such laboratory work is essential to the enduring faithfulness and health of the theological enterprise, consciously or not. Yet, the location of such methodological work often resides at some distance from the muddy trenches of life where Christian faith and ministry take place. In order to connect the nuanced implications of theological method with the practical concerns of life in those trenches, one must have a foot in both arenas, an appreciation for the significance of theological method for Christian faith and ministry, the vision to identify the possible linkages, and the capacity to construct reliable bridges between them.

Chase Davis possesses those four traits and brings them to bear on the question of Christian spiritual formation with insight and accessibility. As a full-time pastor with well-honed theological instincts, he offers an appreciative though critical engagement with an increasingly popular model for spiritual formation presented by James K. A. Smith. Davis's assessment takes place largely at the level of methodology, a type of examination and assessment not often undertaken by Evangelicals, particularly in matters of spiritual formation. Yet, this approach affords the reader the opportunity to understand at a deeper level why an approach like Smith's resonates so deeply and with so many Christians. At the same time, utilizing John Frame's paradigm of Triperspectivalism, Davis shows some areas of Smith's formational paradigm that need closer scrutiny.

This does not result in dismissal of Smith's proposal, but it affords the opportunity to anchor its strengths on more durable epistemological pylons.

"Epistemology" and "spiritual formation" do not often appear in the same sentence. Chase Davis demonstrates how and why they should. The core issues of epistemology—what constitutes knowledge, how we gain knowledge, and how we validate knowledge—have everything to do with what it means to be formed in Christ's image. Every formational strategy seems to have an angle and prioritizes one aspect of human personhood over other aspects; this is understandable to an extent, but always constricting its breadth of effectiveness. James K. A. Smith is keenly aware of this syndrome and he resolute to correct it. Davis brings an epistemological awareness to bear as he analyzes Smith's proposal via John Frame's epistemological method to illuminate the crucial nature of every aspect of the human person in Christian spiritual formation, as well as to honor the legitimacy of every aspect as a starting point for such formation.

For all these reasons, I'm honored to commend Chase Davis's work. His grappling with the epistemology of Christian spiritual formation emerges from a pastor's love for God's people and their spiritual well-being. The fresh set of questions he poses will have portable benefit for the church as those who are gifted and tasked with formational ministries rethink and hone whatever approaches and resources they employ in that grand endeavor.

DON J. PAYNE
Denver Seminary

Preface

CHANGE IS INEVITABLE. I would prefer this not to be true. I would prefer to capture the moments in life when I am happy. When I am watching my boys wrestle and pretend to be superheroes, I wish I could just stop time. But alas, Elon Musk has not made this possible, yet. We will all change. All who are in Christ will be transformed into his likeness (2 Cor 3:18). Being time-bound creatures, change is impossible to fight. Like salmon fighting upstream to reach a place of life, we fight against the current of time, straining and striving to keep things the same. But we know this battle will be lost. Even as we choose to fight time, we are changed by the fight itself, formed into a type of person who resists being changed.

God wants you to change. In fact, Christianity is inherently future oriented, meaning that the inevitability of change is something that should inform our present efforts to develop. Ultimately, God wants to see you changed into the image of his Son (Rom 8:29). He wants you to grow. There are various resources we could use to grow: different methods and strategies to foster the kind of growth God wants. Think of going to Home Depot to search for fertilizer for that house plant you cannot seem to keep alive. There are a variety of options. You could opt for something organic. You could buy something modified with chemicals to help the plant grow. You could entirely replace the house plant every few months and live under the illusion that growth is happening. But there are other considerations.

The context of the plant matters. The oxygen in the air, the heat afforded to the house plant, and the amount of sunlight provided all affect the growth of the houseplant. Not only does context matter, but so does the DNA of the plant itself. Each plant has a different proclivity and propensity to thrive (or not) in different environments. Some plants just do not want to grow.

For many of us who want to know God more and be more like Jesus, we've been told that fertilizer is all we need. Throw some more resources at the problem (prayer, Bible reading, books) and we will grow. And yet we still experience the nagging sense that we are not as healthy as we want to be. We experience the longing for more or what some have called "the torment of the insufficiency of everything attainable."[1] We have the sins that haunt us and the wounds that won't seem to heal. What if there was a better way? At least, this is what I have been wondering. What if the landscape of modern Christianity has been applying solutions that are not working because they are incorrectly diagnosing the problem?

I kept seeing Christians who seemed to have it all together growing up. They didn't seem to struggle with sin. They didn't seem to have doubts. They didn't seem to be bothered by the inconsistencies between what the church practiced and what the Bible taught. And I wanted to know how to live that way; more at peace, not so concerned. But that's not me. That context sent me on a journey to discover what it looks like to be at peace with God, with others, and with myself. To be content with the stage of growth in which I reside. To be at home with myself with God.

The outcome thus-far of that journey is this book. I spent years trying to understand what it meant to grow up into Christ our head (Eph 4:15). I have not arrived by any stretch of the imagination. But, I think I might have discovered an oasis in the desert. The wasteland of discipleship and formation resources is marked by the lives of people who have imploded or flamed out. People who made it part of the way but got tuckered out from the peculiar rat race of American discipleship that pushes us to events, books, and spiritual expectations that we willingly throw on our shoulders.

1. Rolheiser, *Against an Infinite Horizon*, 11.

This is partly to be expected (Mark 4:1–20). We burden ourselves with a yoke we were not meant to bear (Matt 11:29). All the while, God has been beckoning us to a path that few will choose because it seems counter-intuitive; a path that is hard, but the grade is more life giving (Matt 7:13–14). Because ultimately, it is God who carries us. If there is nothing else that you take from this book, know this: it is God alone who saves. Your efforts to change, your desire to change, your Bible reading, prayer, good works, etc., do not add one drop in the ocean of God's love for you. We are justified entirely by the work of Jesus Christ. If our path of change does not begin with God changing us, then our path is doomed. We will be found apart from God because we relied not on him alone but on our efforts to save. This book will be about how to change, but before any of that happens God must change us. He does this by saving us. Then our journey with him will begin from a place of spiritual safety because nothing can separate us from his love (Rom 8:31–29).

My hope in all this spilled ink is that you will know God more and have a vision for what growth could look like for you, your church, your family, and our world. If you feel anything after reading this work, my hope is that it is a sense of relief: relief from the high stakes game many people are playing with Christianity, formation, and discipleship. Relief from self-condemnation towards self and self-righteousness towards others. Relief from the feeling of not measuring up. And maybe enough relief to experience some biblical conviction (not shame) for ways we've missed the mark in what God has for us.

Acknowledgments

THERE ARE MANY PEOPLE who deserve acknowledgement for helping this book come to fruition. My theological advisors and mentors at Denver Seminary, Dr. Don Payne and Dr. David Buschart, were the perfect team to challenge my thinking and sharpen my ideas. The staff and leadership of The Well Church in Boulder, Colorado, have been gracious in providing time for me to complete this work. Thanks are due also to my readers, Dave Morlan and Mason King, for their critical feedback. This work would not have been possible apart from my mom and dad who afforded me opportunities to expand my learning and grow up in a godly home. And finally, thanks are owed to my wife Kim, who has not only encouraged me along the way but has also been faithful to love me as I mature in my thinking, loving, and living.

Introduction

WHAT KIND OF BOOK is this? This book is a theological book. It deals with how we think about and know God. This book is also an academic book. It serves as the completed work of my thesis research and has been reformatted for practitioners of the Christian faith (pastors, professors, church leaders) who are passionate or interested in discipleship and formation. My purpose in this book is to provide a Trinitarian model of formation and discipleship. It is my conviction that many churches offer a version of discipleship that is more akin to a college classroom than the classroom of Jesus Christ. Not only this, but discipleship has become a concept that Evangelicalism has not sufficiently defined. It seems there is a different definition of discipleship for every Christian you might ask to define it. Not to mention, it seems that discipleship (formation) seems to be of minimal importance in many churches when compared to evangelism and church growth strategies. If we can't even agree on a definition, is it any surprise that churches are creating disengaged Christians who can't answer basic questions of Christianity, don't seem to care about Christian ethics, and don't seem to experience the presence of God?

The focus of this work will be the Christian Spiritual Formation (hereafter CSF, or read *discipleship* if you prefer) implications of John Frame's triperspectivalism (read tri-per-spek-tie-vul-ism). Triperspectivalism is a theological method wherein our knowledge of God is informed by three perspectives: the normative, the existential, and the situational. Or, to put it another way, our encounter with ultimate reality is shaped by our reasoning, perceiving, and feeling. These concepts will be further explored and defined in the chapters to follow. The implications of triperspectivalism for formation and discipleship will be explored by placing them in conversation and analysis with James K. A. Smith's theology of formation. It is important to analyze the undergirding beliefs with which Smith approaches formation and discipleship in order to most thoroughly engage his thoughts. Particularly at issue will be an analysis of Smith's epistemic philosophy, which informs his understandings of formation. Epistemic philosophy or epistemology simply means the study of how we know what we know.

This book will contribute to the spiritual health of churches and Christians in two important ways. First, it will demonstrate that the triperspectival method of John Frame is useful not merely for thinking theologically and philosophically, but also for assessing the value of CSF practices. The focus of utilizing triperspectivalism in the realm of CSF has yet to be undertaken, but it is beckoned by Frame and his colleagues.[1] As David Powlison writes, "[c]are and cure of souls represents a further application, an extension, a creative outworking of [Frame's] positive teaching."[2] If triperspectivalism is a valuable tool for examining and analyzing disciple-making strategies and philosophies, then it could have a wide range of applications across Christian ministries committed to fulfilling the great commission.

Imagine an approach to formation and discipleship that is not based in what works best and is most effective (pragmatism), but is instead based in God himself (theology). This is what I believe triperspectivalism offers. Evangelical Christians are passionate about fulfilling the great commission and yet oftentimes lack even a basic common definition of the word *disciple*.[3] One wonders if perhaps we have strayed from the path Jesus has for us if we lack such basic agreement and clarity. An aim of this book is to provide a robustly biblical and Trinitarian understanding of what it means

---

1. Frame, *Doctrine of the Christian Life*, 911.
2. Powlison, "Frame's Ethics," 762.
3. Barna Group, *State of Discipleship*, 9.

to make disciples. This came from my own dissatisfaction in church planting where I could not discern a common definition of discipleship from Evangelical leaders and thinkers.

A second point of emphasis in this book will be a critical engagement with the work of Smith on CSF in a new manner. Smith's thinking on formation is very compelling and popular and this book will provide a critical engagement of his work that will clarify his concept's strengths and weaknesses.[4] While there have been various efforts to critically engage Smith's work, there has yet to be a work that engages his conclusions as drawn from his epistemic beliefs, particularly utilizing a robust theological method such as triperspectivalism.

What is the plan for this work going forward? Well, in order to create a common definition and evaluate whether Smith's work can be considered relevant to CSF, the contemporary landscape of CSF will be explored for such commonalities in the first chapter. We need to define and delineate some categories in order to better understand Smith, just as we would have to prove that Coca-Cola is within the same category (soft drink) as Dr. Pepper before comparing it to (the far superior) Dr. Pepper. Following this, in chapter 2, Frame's triperspectivalism will be explained and explored for strengths and vulnerabilities. This will include a recapitulation (meaning a re-working) of the common definition of CSF into a Framean triad in chapter 3. The idea is to have a baseline understanding of Frame's conception of triperspectivalism and then, based on that definition, see if we can make an iteration for the domain of formation and discipleship. Chapter 4 will take a more detailed look at Smith's philosophy of CSF and the various proposals he makes. Following this, in chapter 5, Smith's philosophy of CSF will be analyzed by the Framean triad developed for such purposes in chapter 3.

Think of it this way; Frame's method, triperspectivalism, is going to be used as a type of magnifying glass through which we will look to see some of the details of Smith's work. This will include areas of agreement and disagreement between Frame and

---

4. Smith, *You Are What You Love.*

Smith in not only their CSF concepts but also their undergirding epistemological assumptions. Finally, a synthesis and proposal for the usefulness and applicability of the Framean CSF triad will be explored to conclude the work in chapters 6 and 7. I have chosen to retain this format of analysis because I believe that by taking two great thinkers of our age, we will have more substantive content to explore rather than just my own thoughts. It is possible that the conclusions drawn in this book could be expanded upon for greater exploration at a later date (as will be suggested in the final chapter).

The aim in all of this work is to propose a theology of formation and discipleship that is doctrinally sound and extremely practical for the church. Triperspectivalism provides a rich Trinitarian framework for thinking theologically. This framework can be built upon and developed into a vision for formation and discipleship for churches to more faithfully and effectively obey Jesus's command to make disciples. This book is an attempt to create a common definition based on one the most foundational Christian doctrines—the Trinity—to help churches and people obey the command to make disciples.

CHAPTER 1

Defining Formation
and Discipleship

NAVIGATING WAS MY FAVORITE part of the drive. When I was a kid, my family would make an annual pilgrimage to Colorado. One of the best things about this family road trip was getting to play navigator. No doubt my dad had memorized the route, but he would ask me for directions while I helped by opening the road atlas that was bigger than me. Looking at the entire picture of our road trip gave me a better idea of where we were going and what it would take to get there. The aim of this first chapter is to provide a similar scope. If we are going to understand the importance of the work of John Frame and James Smith and how they relate, then we need to begin by exploring the terrain and be sure they are on the same map.

Jesus expects that his people will go about making disciples (Matt 28:19). However, being two-thousand years removed from the context of Jesus's day and the means by which one made disciples then, how are we to understand this command today? Seeing this command as a command of Christian spiritual formation will expand the opportunities for applying what Jesus meant when he said, "Make disciples." However, in order to see these opportunities, we first need to clarify what is meant when we say Christian spiritual formation (CSF).

CONTEMPORARY FIELD OF DISCOURSE IN CSF

Spiritual formation has to do with the means and theories by which we go about developing our spiritual life.[1] It deals with methods, habits, ideas, and concepts that as a composite picture define our spiritual life. CSF is concerned with the end goal of our spiritual life and also the development of our spiritual life along the way. It is not only teleological in nature, but also practical. Meaning, it does not just focus on the destination and purpose of formation but also how we get there. The destination and the journey are both important. In spiritual formation, we do not just focus on the ends but also the means to those ends. Just as a sailor is concerned about how to reach her final port of call, so too she is concerned about knowing where that port is located. Likewise, we should be concerned not only with the final vision of what it looks like to be formed, but also the methods and means of how to get there. CSF is concerned with the development of a spiritual life along the way of becoming mature in Christ (Jas 1:2–4).

In some ways, we can think of CSF as concerning "pilgrims— Christians, being on a journey to become more Christian."[2] In Mark Maddix's understanding, CSF has to do with the journey, what some call discipleship, of following and learning from Jesus and being formed into his character and likeness in our capacities (Eph 4:15). CSF is not just about methods and concepts regarding formation, but also about the discovery of methods and concepts. It deals with the acquisition of knowledge and how we come to understand the truth of the gospel. It deals with how we learn. This is crucial to understand. Discipleship and formation do not just deal with tools and methods, they deal with growth and maturity. At the heart of growth and maturity is the ability to learn and know. In this way, CSF will invariably address issues of epistemology. Epistemology is how we know what we know. This topic will be thoroughly examined later, but suffice it to say that CSF must deal with how we know anything at all.

---

1. Boa, *Conformed to His Image*, 21.
2. Maddix, "Spiritual Formation and Christian Formation," 241.

Unfortunately, some Christians have given into "the dichotomous default" in formation and discipleship, where "passion and faith have been linked to relationship and theology has been linked to knowledge."[3] In this understanding, questions of philosophy and knowledge are relegated to the academy rather than being the bread and butter of disciple-making activities. This is an unfortunate philosophical holdover from the Enlightenment. In this conception of formation, two things that should be held together, relationship and theology, are separated because of the modern conception that relationships deal with emotion and passion rather than "knowledge."

Some posit that CSF deals with the inner life primarily (think words like *soul* or *spirit*). The Christian formation thinker Dallas Willard posits that spiritual formation is "the process by which the human spirit or will is given a definite 'form' or character."[4] This form or character has to do with lived out obedience, beliefs, and desires. He also argues that "*the body lies right at the center of the spiritual life*."[5] However, Willard emphasizes most directly that it is the "inner life that counts" in spiritual formation.[6] The soul is the focus of spiritual formation. There is a tension in Willard's writing in this regard. For Willard, the body takes on the composition of the inner life and "becomes a major part of the hidden source from which our life immediately flows."[7] Furthermore, he believes that "in vain do we try to change people's hearts or character by moving them to do things in ways that bypass their understanding."[8] In this scheme, it is the inner life of people that formation must first address.

---

3. Meek, *Loving to Know*, 139.

4. Willard, *Renovation of the Heart*, 19. The relationship of the body to spiritual formation will be a recurring topic throughout because both Frame and Smith discuss it.

5. Willard, *Renovation of the Heart*, 159. Italics original. Willard's conviction reflects an Augustinian anthropology in which human composition is understood to be dichotomous (soul and body). In this schema, the soul is held in higher regard than the body.

6. Willard, *Renovation of the Heart*, 24.

7. Willard, *Renovation of the Heart*, 165.

8. Willard, *Great Omission*, 194.

A main feature of this understanding of spiritual formation is the primacy of the intellect in formation. For Willard, and others who approach CSF from his perspective, cognitive propositional teaching must come before heart and behavioral change can take place. Jeff Vanderstelt's approach exemplifies this understanding when he claims that "*santification* is just a big word for becoming more and more *like* Jesus through faith *in* Jesus. You *become* like what you *believe in*."[9] In other words, belief is the starting point for transformation. In order for someone to stop an addiction, for example, they must be taught something. For many Evangelicals, teaching forms the bedrock of formation. In many respects, this approach to formation mirrors the field of cognitive behavioral therapy.[10] Elsewhere, Willard personally reflects and concedes that he

> had been raised in religious circles of very fine people where the emphasis had been exclusively on faithfulness to right beliefs and upon bringing others to profess those beliefs. Now, that, of course, is of central importance. But when that *alone* is emphasized, the result is a dry and powerless religious life, no matter how sincere, and one constantly vulnerable to temptations of all kinds.[11]

When intellect becomes the sole focus and emphasis of formation, it can result in malformed and undernourished disciples.

A common tension within the discipline of CSF you might be sensing at this point is the relationship between the body and soul in forming people. The tension manifests itself in nitty-gritty details regarding how people's bodies impact their souls and *vice versa*.[12] Even the title of spiritual formation (CSF) lends itself towards confusion as it seems to focus only on the inner or immaterial spiritual life of the soul. Furthermore, there is a tension between methods

---

9. Vanderstelt, *Gospel Fluency*, 21.

10. In fact, it could be argued that preaching and teaching ministries have so borrowed the philosophical concepts of cognitive behavioral therapy that they are nearly indistinguishable in their formational purposes. This could, in part, explain the rise of moralistic therapeutic deism in American society.

11. Willard, *Great Omission*, 217.

12. This also surfaces the tension between the mind and body commonly referred to as the mind-body problem.

and concepts of spiritual development and necessary external change which should correspond with the development of the soul. Many Christians are leery of any formation that sounds like behavior modification before heart change. Heart change is king according to Evangelical folk theology. As Willard points out, "spiritual disciplines are not primarily for the solving of behavioral problems, though that is one of their effects."[13] The result of spiritual disciplines that focus on the interior and immaterial is material change. He believes that "the aim of disciplines in the spiritual life . . . is the transformation of the total state of the soul," not just behavioral change.[14] Willard believes that behavior and knowledge are insufficient *foci* for the transformation of people. However, it is at times unclear in Willard's writing what he suggests as a comprehensive way forward in resolving the tension between the body and soul in CSF because of the nature of his Augustinian theological anthropology. Augustine, a third-century Christian theologian, tended to elevate the soul above the body in terms of spiritual importance. This Platonic dualism approach to the material and immaterial has haunted Christian perspectives on formation and discipleship. Reflect upon how much the songs in our churches, the emphasis in our preaching, and the methods of our discipleship minimize the embodied experience and elevate the immaterial. Even the word *spiritual* has come to be commonly understood as synonymous with the immaterial. The tension centers on the elevation of the immaterial as the primary and more significant of the material and immaterial realities of each person.

Some attempt to navigate the tension between the body and soul by placing a primary emphasis on affections and desires as the starting point for formation. Eugene Peterson, another thought leader of Christian spirituality, points out that "many think that the only way to change your behavior is to first change your feelings."[15] However, he counters that "we are psychosomatic beings; body and

---

13. Willard, *Great Omission*, 151.

14. Willard, *Great Omission*, 151.

15. Peterson, *Long Obedience*, 194.

spirit are intricately interrelated."[16] Biblically speaking, behavior can precede and inform feelings according to Peterson. However, when we begin to demand that behavior comes before our soul is properly attended to the behavior, we can be in dangerous waters. This can easily lead to a type of performance in the worst sense of the word. As David Clark points out, "the 'think and obey' approach to spiritual formation can too easily lead to outward forms of conforming religiosity that leave the human heart in a state of decay."[17] This concern is mirrored in Michael Wilkins work, as he states that "external actions are an indication of a heart that is rightly directed toward Jesus, and those actions are accomplished by the inner working of God in response to faith."[18]

Despite the focus on the inner life, as Willard states above, discipleship and formation almost always get played out behaviorally, or they involve our embodied existence. Spiritual formation typically consists of spiritual disciplines that are intended to cultivate a greater connection to God (Rom 12:2). In spiritual formation, we help people attend to themselves, assess themselves accurately (Rom 12:3), and provide for them a safe place "in which self-evaluation can take place."[19] As traditionally understood, in Evangelical spiritual formation, we help people cultivate character by focusing on higher-order things prior to the actual behaviors to be changed. When one wants to address aberrant behavior, the typical prescription is more Bible reading and church attendance. Struggle with anger at your kids? Read a book on anger. Listen to a sermon on anger. Memorize twenty verses on anger. That way, godly understanding can produce change. As mentioned previously, this more Augustinian understanding of human personhood and the development of one's spiritual life is common in Evangelicalism. This view of personhood and development warrants further investigation and will be explored in subsequent chapters.

16. Peterson, *Long Obedience*, 194.

17. Clark, *To Know and Love God*, 421.

18. Wilkins, *Following the Master*, 220.

19. Moreland, "Spiritual Formation and the Nature of the Soul," 42.

Spiritual formation typically deals with how people are fully restored in their humanity (Eph 2:4–10). In fact, the vision of God in formation is that we would become more human. The way we become more human is by relationally knowing God through Jesus God. According to Jim Cofield and Rich Plass, CSF occurs from a foundational "receptive, participatory, relational experience with the receptive, relational God."[20] It is not about earning our way to connection with God but instead becoming more aware of his initiatory presence in our lives through our union with Christ and the indwelling of the Holy Spirit. This can be cultivated through practices that develop a responsiveness to God's presence. It is important to note that we are not speaking of the inherent value and dignity of humans but instead the capabilities of people to connect to God and glorify him. Human capacities and the development of those capacities do not diminish the worth or value of anyone. Formation should engage such capabilities and capacities. CSF does not assume that people are fundamentally rational, instead that they are fundamentally personal. This means that people are not just creatures that can think. We are relational and designed for relationship. Personhood is by nature fundamentally interpersonal.[21] Our very personhood is constituted in relationships with others, both God and man.

Where does this leave us? As has been shown, formation and discipleship deals with both the material and immaterial realities of people's lives. CSF can be defined as *approaches to spirituality that are distinctly rooted in the Christian faith and seek to form our material and immaterial capacities in their ability to connect with God and glorify him in life.* In this definition, we have a summary of a variety of perspectives that have been explored. Because the argument of this book is that Frame's triperspectivalism provides a biblically and theologically rich approach to formation, this summary definition will be used to explore triperspectivalism. A tension arises at this point, however. Frame is a theologian and triperspectivalism is a theological method by which Frame does theology. Issues of

20. Plass and Cofield, *Relational* Soul, 91.

21. Meek, *Loving to Know*, 220.

discipleship and formation are not commonly thought of as conversant with theological studies. As an example, it could be akin to taking a lure intended to catch bass and fishing for trout (something for which the lure was not intended). However, CSF is a discipline within theology, even if not traditionally represented as such within that field of study. It is typically relegated to sections of bookstores and bookshelves dealing with Christian living and more practical matters. Its warranted inclusion and its particular significance in theology proper will be explored next. This is important because both Frame and Smith are theologians and we must verify that we are swimming in the same pond.

CHRISTIAN SPIRITUAL FORMATION
SITUATED THEOLOGICALLY

We need to be certain that CSF is in fact a theological category because this book is a theological book and not just a book on spiritual formation. CSF is a major component of the theological enterprise. Its significance is often overlooked or overshadowed because it does not fit in traditional theological categories. Instead, CSF blends several theological disciplines and their underlying convictions into practical applications. Think of how a whale swims in the water and yet is classified as a mammal. By all appearances, it should be an amphibian, but it is a mammal. Similarly, matters of formation and discipleship are often mistaken as issues of Christian living and not traditional categories on par with ecclesiology and soteriology. CSF is informed by doctrine and epistemology and reflects an amalgamation of theological disciplines. While CSF does not get much attention from theologians writing systematic and biblical theologies, it is extremely relevant to the discipline of theology. Let's examine this claim more by showing how CSF relates to several theological categories.

Sanctification deals with CSF in the sense that sanctification is defined as the spiritual transformation of people. As traditionally understood by most Evangelicals, sanctification has to do with growth in holiness. Some think of sanctification with regard to "the continuing work of God in the life of believers, making them actually holy."[22] In other words, sanctification has to do with growing in holiness. John Frame describes sanctification as "God's work to make us holy."[23] While most theologians refer to sanctification as growth in godliness or holiness, it could be more appropriate to refer to this process of development as transformation rather than sanctification biblically.[24] Because CSF consists of approaches to spirituality that are distinctly rooted in the Christian faith and seeks to form our material and immaterial capacities in their ability to connect with God and glorify him in life, CSF is inherently related to the theological discipline of sanctification wherein theologians discuss growing in godliness or perfection.[25]

CSF also deals with theological concepts related to anthropology. Theological anthropology deals with two main theological concepts. First, theological anthropology deals with human composition. That is, of what parts or components are people made: Are we body and soul? Are we body, soul, and spirit? Are we simply material bodies? Human composition deals with biblical conclusions regarding the immaterial (typically referred to as soul, mind, or spirit) and material (typically referred to as body) aspects of humanity. Theological anthropology is an inevitable topic of conversation when talking about CSF, as has been shown with Willard's approach.

Second, theological anthropology deals with the theological concept of the *imago Dei*. The *imago Dei* deals with the value and dignity of people being made in the image of God. As John Kilner argues, "Creation *in* God's image is God's expressed *intention* that people evidence the special connection they have with God through a meaningful relationship with God."[26] With this working definition, CSF deals with restoring the connection to God that all people are intended to have. Therefore, CSF is intricately connected to theological anthropology.

---

22. Erickson, *Christian Theology*, 897.

23. Frame, *Systematic Theology*, 983.

24. Payne, *Already Sanctified*.

25. Noble, *Holy Trinity*, 42–43.

26. Kilner, *Dignity and* Destiny, 79.

The first move in CSF is a connection to God in faith or trust and repentance because at the heart of knowing God is trust.[27] This is only possible through Jesus Christ. While CSF can be utilized prior to a saving knowledge of God, it will not serve its intended purpose because it is designed to operate with a connection to God as the starting point. However, CSF can be useful to help people explore Christianity and position them to examine or question their own relationship with God. In fact, CSF can be used as an evangelistic tool to help people with no connection to God in Jesus Christ to begin to explore the various longings of their lives and how they could find satisfaction in Christ.

CSF also deals with theological concepts related to ecclesiology. Ecclesiology deals with the essential nature, purpose, and practices of the church universal and local. Since the church is God's plan for the expansion of his kingdom and the formation of disciples, CSF is a related discipline to ecclesiology. Because formation has communal implications as it is interpersonal and much of formation is created by and for churches, CSF is an integral component of any ecclesiological exercise. The church exists as an outpost of the kingdom and its mission is derivative of the mission of God or the *Missio Dei*. It has no existence apart from God's prior redemptive purposes. Churches do not own the mission of God, they are stewards of his mission. If a main emphasis of this stewarded mission is to make disciples, then CSF should be of paramount concern within ecclesiological studies. Not only this, but CSF intersects with both theological anthropology and ecclesiology because CSF deals with people made in God's image who are communal. Based on the intrinsic communal nature of personhood, the church provides the preeminent and God-ordained context for CSF to take place. God established the church as the people where relational wounds can be healed relationally.

Furthermore, building on ecclesiology, CSF deals with theological concepts related to discipleship and mission. Discipleship and mission have to do with a variety of topics related to conversion, ecclesiology, sanctification, evangelism, pneumatology, and

---

27. Meek, *Loving to Know*, 14.

theology proper with God's purposes in the world. Because CSF deals with the formation of people in their connection with God, it is related to discipleship as traditionally understood in Evangelical theologies. Dallas Willard comments on this by saying that "discipleship means living interactively with his resurrected presence (through his word, his personal presence, and through other people) as we progressively learn *to lead our lives as he would if he were we*."[28] James K. A. Smith himself makes the argument that discipleship and formation are related in concluding that "discipleship is more a matter of hungering and thirsting than of knowing and believing."[29]

Discipleship does not receive treatment as a traditional theological field of study, but it does deal with many aspects of CSF. Discipleship, biblically speaking, has to do with equipping people to follow God in their lives. Wilkins defines a disciple of Jesus as "one who has come to Jesus for eternal life, has claimed him as Savior and God, and has embarked upon the life of following him."[30] He further describes the journey of discipleship as all-encompassing and holistic over human life.[31] While it is outside the scope of this book, it could be argued that what is now called CSF more closely resembles a biblical understanding of discipleship than many of the discipleship resources and teaching in modern Evangelicalism. Or as I have heard one professor put it, "everything commonly associated with 'spiritual formation' is actually part of discipleship."[32] I could not agree more with this sentiment. Wilkins makes a case that "we need to move toward a more integrative understanding" of discipleship.[33] This more integrative understanding, I would propose, is called Christian spiritual formation.

28. Willard, *Great Omission*, 166. Italics original.

29. Smith, *You Are What You Love*, 2.

30. Wilkins, *Following the Master*, 342.

31. Wilkins, *Following the Master*, 125; 342.

32. Donald Payne, Associate Professor of Theology and Christian Formation at Denver Seminary, in email to the author, March 6, 2019.

33. Wilkins, *Following the Master*, 346. In this regard, a byproduct of this thesis is to develop a more integrative approach by corresponding discipleship and CSF.

Discipleship should not just have a singular focus on cognitive transformation but instead should be a holistic approach to making people more human. Richard Longenecker summarizes that in the New Testament, discipleship themes consist of self-understanding, imitation, "authentic Christian experience," and practice.[34] In this way, discipleship becomes a journey of discovery. Esther Lightcap Meek argues from an epistemological point of view that "discipleship and religious formation are far better understood as a 'being on the way to knowing.'"[35] By this, she means that knowledge is more about transformation than information.[36] Al Mohler, president of the Southern Baptist Theological Seminary, exemplified a common understanding of discipleship by recently stating that "discipleship is about teaching Christians how we are to live holy lives in a fallen world."[37] This teaching, according to Mohler, comes from the Bible. This highlights a very common Evangelical understanding that discipleship has to do with propositional truths communicated from the Bible to people. However, discipleship has implications for all of life, not simply the traditional understanding of truth as propositional teaching.

With the wide range of topics which CSF covers, including but not limited to sanctification, anthropology, ecclesiology, and discipleship and mission, it is easy to see that CSF is a theological category worthy of theological reflection. If we are going to draw from theologians and philosophers as contributors to CSF, then we needed to clarify that CSF falls within the scope of their influence. Tesla, being an electric car, falls under the legal code for automobiles in most respects. Teslas are different than traditional automobiles, but they are still automobiles. Christian spiritual formation is different from traditional categories of theology, but it is a theological topic.

Attention still needs to be given to Smith's writing on CSF so as to situate his works within this theological genre. If CSF is a

---

34. Longenecker, *Patterns of Discipleship*, 5.

35. Meek, *Loving to Know*, 40.

36. Meek, *Loving to Know*, 63.

37. Mohler, "Part II: To be cool or to be a church?"

theological topic, we need to be sure that Smith is writing on this topic if we are going to engage with his work.

JAMES K. A. SMITH'S WRITINGS ON CSF

Christian faithfulness in the postmodern world faces extensive challenges in terms of identity, formation, and thinking. The sheer quantity of technological changes alone in the last hundred years presents significant issues in Christian formation and education. Consumer culture in our world lures people into thinking that to consume is to be human. Modern and postmodern philosophies present new opportunities for discovery but also turn formation into a buffet of identity options. It is into these challenges and issues that James K. A. Smith steps. Recently, Smith has written specifically on the topic of spiritual formation within Evangelical Christianity. While not traditionally categorized as dealing with CSF, much of his work deals with the topics related to CSF. His work has been categorized with regard to philosophy, theology, and even worldview and ecclesiology. However, much of his work comes down to issues of CSF and theological anthropology. The thrust of his philosophical convictions is played out ecclesiologically by discussing the best practices for CSF within churches. That is, Smith writes on church life and how it affects people. While his theological anthropology and epistemology will be briefly addressed, the purpose of interacting with his material is to deal with his thoughts surrounding CSF.

A primary work that will be utilized for careful understanding of Smith's ideas will be *You Are What You Love*.[38] In this work, he argues that modern contemporary Christian formation and discipleship methods have ignored cultural liturgies as the primary vehicle for formation.[39] Smith defines cultural liturgies as those practices that draw out our affections and desires. Think of how a football or basketball game surfaces our loyalties. I may deny that I am a Dallas Cowboys fan all I want, but when the game is on the line, they are my team. My affections are revealed. Smith argues that "our

38. Smith, *You Are What You Love*.
39. Smith, *You Are What You Love*, 22–23.

desires are caught more than they are taught."[40] Because the church has neglected to acknowledge and act on these realities (cultural liturgies and the importance of desire in formation), it has truncated formation mainly into an intellectual enterprise. In his estimation, formation has been reduced to having a Christian worldview with right beliefs. Smith argues that the church is losing the cultural battle because it is not tapping into Christian formational patterns of liturgies. Secular cultural liturgies are winning because we have become inoculated to their prevalence and dominance in our desires.[41] Like a fish in water, we don't know anything other than secular liturgies because we live so completely within it. He suggests that instead of addressing formation from a perspective of worldview and the impartation of propositional truth, we must adapt our methods to address the affections and practices of people.

Smith's series, called *Cultural Liturgies*, will also been drawn upon in this book. In this series, he provides a more robust argument of his basic thesis in *You Are What You Love*.[42] He also provides a way forward for the church (and other educational institutions) to reorient its formational methods towards a more holistic and, what he calls, "gut level" discipleship.[43] By this, Smith means formation and discipleship that taps into desire as a primary concern before the intellect. Our aim, according to Smith, should be the heart before the head. While *You Are What You Love* provides Smith's most approachable and hence most popular rendition of his convictions, *Cultural Liturgies* provides a more in-depth analysis: "[W]orship, and not worldviews, is the key to Christian education and the formation of students who will desire the kingdom of God."[44] For Smith, many contemporary Evangelical methods of formation (read discipleship) focus exclusively on worldview formation that deals with the intellect or mind. The emphasis is more on the transmission of propositional truth claims to people or worldviews.

---

40. Smith, *You Are What You Love*, 22.
41. Smith, *Desiring the Kingdom*, 85.
42. Smith, *Cultural Liturgies*; Smith, *You Are What You Love*.
43. Smith, *Imagining the Kingdom*, 127.
44. Thiessen, "Review," 48.

Instead of worldview, Smith believes that worship and affections are most important in the formation of people. Tawa Anderson summarizes this:

> Smith argues that humans are inherently liturgical creatures; if we do not worship God (through Christian liturgies), then we will engage in secular liturgies that set something else up as the object of worship. Hence, Christian education needs to be formative, not just informative—shaping loves, not just teaching us what to love. Accordingly, Smith insists, worldview education is inadequate; we are creatures of desire and imagination, not of thought or belief.[45]

In this sense, Smith's work is very concerned with CSF philosophy and practice.

These are some of the core themes in much of Smith's work, particularly in the first two volumes of his cultural liturgies series as well as *You Are What You Love.* If CSF deals with *approaches to spirituality that are distinctly rooted in the Christian faith and seek to form our material and immaterial capacities in their ability to connect with God and glorify him in life,* then Smith's writings are works of CSF. While his works may have more a philosophical orientation, there can be no doubt that a major emphasis for him is on the formation of people.

Furthermore, Smith deals with theological anthropology in order to bolster his central thesis that worship is more fundamental than worldview formation in shaping the desires of people. Worship, for Smith, is best understood to mean the practices that shape our affections.[46] This is in contrast to popular understandings of worship that are described as reflecting our affections rather than shaping them. Think of how we commonly consider worship music. Our primary concern is if the words and music reflect our beliefs and not the other way around. Smith believes that people are a type of higher animal and subsequently this anthropological conviction justifies instinctual worship. This means that worship is

---

45. T. Anderson, "Imagining the Kingdom," 187.
46. Smith, *You Are What You Love,* 23.

more primal than it is thoughtful. Rather than people being of a different order than animals, we are simply more developed animals that still operate mainly by instinct.[47]

Smith's works also deal with ecclesiology. Much of his writing is pitched as an apologetic for high liturgy (meaning Christian church services and academic settings that are more traditional: think Catholic, Anglican, Presbyterian, and Methodist). In his understanding, liturgies are those practices which churches utilize to cultivate an awareness of God.[48] Smith believes that in order to combat the liturgies of the world and modern consumerism, churches must develop more robust liturgies that tap into the gut level affections of people in order to shape their desires. Smith's solution to bad spiritual formation is to provide a robust liturgy that reshapes the desires of people. This liturgy would tell the story of the gospel in a way that people could grow in their material and immaterial capacities to glorify God more. Rather than teaching propositional truth claims as a fundamental means of formation, as is exemplified in many (if not most) Evangelical churches, Smith sees better liturgy as the first step in the formation of people.

Smith's work *Who's Afraid of Relativism?* serves as the foundational philosophical framework for his *Cultural Liturgies* series (as he himself admits) and describes his epistemological convictions.[49] This may seem too philosophical at first, but do not miss this point. Smith has given us his philosophy of formation in a book on philosophy. His perspective on formation is rooted in his understanding of epistemology. This then informs his work in *Cultural Liturgies*, which articulates his convictions regarding theological anthropology and CSF. *You Are What You Love* then serves as the more accessible and therefore popular work summarizing his philosophy of CSF. It is important to look at Smith's *Who's Afraid of Relativism?* because it serves as the starting point for his more popular writings on CSF. This is very telling and helpful in understanding the more practical implications of his theories. In this work,

---

47. Smith, *Desiring the Kingdom,* 28; Smith, *You Are What You Love,* 33.

48. Smith, *You Are What You Love,* 23.

49. Smith, *Who's Afraid of Relativism?,* 152–23.

Smith summarizes his position by building on George Lindbeck, a postliberal scholar who believed that doctrine was defined by the community that possessed it rather than external sources such as Scripture.[50] David Clark describes Lindbeck's position as a narrative position that seeks to reclaim the importance of context and community in epistemology. However, he warns that "narrativism offers a crucial but one-sided warning. The warning is valid but also needs balance."[51] With Lindbeck, context and community determine doctrine prior to Scripture.

In Smith's estimation, Lindbeck is the theologian *par excellence* with regard to the implications of a pragmatic relativistic epistemological framework in the church.[52] As Smith notes:

> discipleship, then, is a kind of acculturation: to become religious involved becoming skilled in the language, the symbol system of a given religion. To become a Christian involves learning the story of Israel and of Jesus well enough to interpret and experience oneself and one's world in its terms.[53]

In this way, discipleship resembles more an ancient catechumenate whereby neophytes were invited to join a way of life and allegiance to Jesus Christ, not just to subscribe to certain propositional truths.[54] Formation is an introduction into a new pond rather than trying to teach fish how to walk.

As has been demonstrated in this chapter, Smith's thinking and recent writings are, if anything, works of CSF. They deal with the same issues as Evangelical concepts of CSF. This chapter has also demonstrated that CSF is a theological category deserving of analysis from a theological lens. Not only this, but a working definition of CSF has been established so as to be useful in the remainder of this book. This definition is important because it should serve as a

---

50. Smith pulls from *The Nature of Doctrine*, Lindbeck's most significant work, in order to summarize his position.

51. Clark, *To Know and Love God*, 48.

52. Smith, *Who's Afraid of Relativism?*, 152.

53. Lindbeck, *Nature of Doctrine*, 34; Smith, *Who's Afraid of Relativism?*, 159.

54. Smith, *Who's Afraid of Relativism?*, 176.

common definition of formation and discipleship. Therefore, here it is again: *CSF (discipleship) consists of approaches to spirituality that are distinctly rooted in the Christian faith and seek to form our material and immaterial capacities in their ability to connect with God and glorify him in life.* Because Evangelicalism lacks a consistent definition of discipleship and formation, this proposed definition, which is an amalgamation of various Evangelical theological traditions, will serve as a type of blueprint. This will allow us to develop a model of discipleship that both honors the common understanding of formation in Evangelicalism while at the same time improving it.

If we are going to have fully formed disciples of Jesus, we need to make sure that we agree on what formation and discipleship entail. We must be clear on the definition and the problem if we are going to be clear on how to obey the command to make disciples. Thus far, we have simply set the table in order to see if common tensions within spiritual formation and discipleship can be resolved by utilizing triperspectivalism, which is the argument of this book. By establishing a common definition of CSF and showing its relevance to theological studies, we can explore the relationship between CSF and triperspectivalism. How might triperspectivalism help our efforts in making disciples? It is to this task we turn next.

CHAPTER 2

Triperspectivalism as a Theological Method

"MAKE SURE YOU ADDRESS the ball the right way." This is what I heard my dad say often when he taught me to play golf. "Addressing the ball" has to do with your stance and approach to the task of hitting the ball. In golf, the way in which one lines up to hit the shot has serious consequences for the direction the ball will take. The manner in which we approach a topic as significant as discipleship has significant consequences as well. Because discipleship is typically approached pragmatically (what one does) instead of philosophically (what it is and why), discipleship and formation often lacks a significant theological underpinning. Triperspectivalism offers a robust and theologically rich philosophical approach to discipleship and formation. But what is triperspectivalism?

As a primary source for defining John Frame's definition of triperspectivalism, this book will engage his most recent work, *Theology in Three Dimensions*, in which he explains his understanding and utilization of triperspectivalism as a theological method.[1] If triperspectivalism can be utilized in the way this book aims to use it, then really homing in on a clear understanding of

---

1. Frame, *Theology in Three Dimensions*, 2017.

triperspectivalism is crucial. Triperspectivalism, as mentioned in the introduction, is a theological method and an epistemological approach which takes into account three ways of knowing ultimate reality: reasoning, perceiving, and feeling.[2] Triperspectivalism can be thought of as a pedagogical or teaching tool. It is a tool to help people learn and thereby grow. Frame describes triperspectivalism as "a teaching tool to help us grasp some of the deep things in Scripture."[3] For Frame, triperspectivalism is a tool to help people understand theological concepts. It is a theological method he utilizes prolifically and, for someone who first encounters this method, it can be daunting.[4] Frame's work, *Systematic Theology*, also employs and describes triperspectivalism, and therefore it will be drawn from to articulate his understanding of triperspectivalism.[5] After establishing an understanding for and assessing the viability of triperspectivalism, a CSF integration triad will be provided through which James K. A. Smith will be analyzed in order to test the triad's durability. What we want to do is build a tool to analyze various philosophies of CSF. Much like an X-ray machine is able to see through tissue and get to the bones, a CSF tool of analysis should be able to see in such a way as to discover the various epistemic components of a philosophy of CSF.

DEFINITION OF TRIPERSPECTIVALISM

A definition for triperspectivalism can be difficult to nail down, as Timothy Miller points out, because John Frame defines "meaning as use."[6] What does "meaning as use" mean? This means that the definition of triperspectivalism is best explored through *use* rather than through a *propositional definition*. When I was in high school, I had a football coach who would ask if we packed our lunch pail

---

2. Frame, *Theology in Three Dimensions*, 1120. Also the normative, the existential, and the situational.

3. Frame, *Theology in Three Dimensions*, x.

4. Frame lists around one hundred triads in his systematic theology.

5. Frame, *Systematic Theology*.

6. Miller, *Triune God*, 37–97.

and brought our ladder at pep rallies. For this coach, he was referring to coal mining days when people would pack a lunch and bring
a ladder to work. Our coach was asking us if we were ready to get
to work. The definition of the concept was defined by its use in the
pep rally. It was "meaning as use." This is how Frame suggests we
understand triperspectivalism, by looking at how it is used.

Where did Frame develop this theological method? A starting
point would be Frame's "theological methodology of multiperspectivalism," which was introduced in 1987 by his work *Doctrine of the
Knowledge of God.*[7] However, Frame often shows that the concept
of triperspectivalism can be traced biblically and theologically to
both the reality and philosophy of the Trinity itself. The Trinity is
a foundational and yet under-appreciated Christian doctrine for
most people. While Frame's own enthusiasm regarding the Trinitarian origins of triperspectivalism is at times muted and other
times inconsistent, there is no doubt that it has Trinitarian roots.[8]
Because the Trinity is one of the greatest mysteries in Christianity,
one might be tempted to simply call the three persons of the Trinity three perspectives as a way of better understanding it. Frame
quickly dismisses this as a possibility due the charge of a heresy
called Sabellianism: "the idea that the differences of the person are
merely differences in the way we look at the one God."[9] This means
that God would have three faces that he shows at different times.
This heresy was battled and disavowed in the early church. Frame
does however state that "if the three persons are not *mere* perspectives on the Godhead, they nevertheless *are* perspectives. They are
more than perspectives, but not less."[10] Think of how an airplane is
a vehicle, but the word vehicle does not really do justice to what an
airplane can do. An airplane is not a mere vehicle, but it is a vehicle,
nonetheless. In a similar way, the persons of the Trinity are perspectives, but not just perspectives.

---

7. Torres, "Perspectives on Multiperspectivalism," 111.

8. Miller, *Triune God of Unity,* 111.

9. Frame, "Primer on Perspectivalism."

10. Frame, "Primer on Perspectivalism."

Historically speaking, versions of triperspectivalism have been used by other theologians in church history. For example, John Calvin thought in a way congruent to triperspectivalism in the way that he described the three offices of Christ: prophet, priest, and king.[11] This is true not only of Calvin, but also of other Reformed confessions and theological documents.[12] In recent years, it has been Frame who popularized triperspectivalism as a theological method.

For Frame, triperspectivalism is grounded in the Lordship of God, or what he refers to as God's lordship attributes. God's lordship attributes are seen in the Trinity: "the Father acts as *supreme authority* within the Trinity, establishing the eternal plan that the other persons bring into effect."[13] The Son serves as the "*executive power* of the Trinity."[14] By this, Frame means to say that the Son is responsible for accomplishing what God the Father has planned. Third, "the Spirit is the *pervasive presence* of the Trinity in all things."[15] These three things, God's supreme authority, his executive powers, and his pervasive presence "describe the ways in which God rules the creation."[16] These three concepts serve as the theological backdrop for the use of his theological method triperspectivalism. Triperspectivalism is, if anything, Trinitarian.

Triperspectivalism is grounded in Trinitarian relationality. As Meek summarizes:

> Frame claims that God's Lordship consists of his control, his authority, and his presence. God has authority: he has the right to be Lord. God controls all things, and so is Lord. And God is everywhere present, and thus is Lord. To know God the covenant Lord, then, is to know his authority (expressed in his law), his control (in his

---

11. Calvin, *Institutes*, 494.

12. Frame, "Primer on Perspectivalism."

13. Frame, *Theology in Three Dimensions*, 19. Italics original.

14. Frame, *Theology in Three Dimensions*, 19. Italics original.

15. Frame, *Theology in Three Dimensions*, 19. Italics original.

16. Frame, *Theology in Three Dimensions*, 19.

works, i.e., the world), and his presence (in ourselves as knowers).[17]

These three themes of control, authority, and presence are mentioned throughout Frame's systematic, as highlighted by Meek:

> There is also an obvious correspondence between these and the three Persons of the Trinity: the Father, authority (the Father gives the Law); the Son, control (his incarnation brings him into the world, among us); the Holy Spirit, presence (his ministry is God within us).[18]

According to Frame, triperspectivalism is not just another theological method but the most theologically faithful theological method as it is founded on the very nature of the Godhead. There is a perichoretic relationship in triperspectivalism just as there in the Trinity.[19] Meaning that in the Trinity each person experiences relational connectedness and exchange with one another. There is a mutuality within the Trinity. Think of how a husband and wife are two and yet one. Similarly, with the Trinity, there are three in one.

Triperspectivalism is also a variation of multiperspectivalism as pointed about by Miller.[20] Miller shows that there are generally "two major types of perspectivalism, which we will call *general perspectivalism* and *triperspectivalism*."[21] General perspectivalism is the idea that there are multiple perspectives to any approach to knowledge.[22] It "describes the implications of the epistemological fact that humans come to knowledge by means of various points of view."[23] Think of how you get to know another person. You can know them through interpersonal communication, through studying their resume, through looking at their Instagram account, through knowing where they live, through completing a project

---

17. Meek, *Loving to Know,* 158.

18. Meek, *Loving to Know,* 159.

19. Miller, *Triune God of Unity,* 184–86.

20. Miller, "Theological Method," 34.

21. Miller, "Theological Method," 35.

22. Miller, *Triune God of Unity,* 31.

23. Miller, *Triune God of Unity,* 32.

with them, or through sharing a meal with them. There are multiple ways people approach knowing. Triperspectivalism is more explicit in that it emphasizes three focal points in our engagement with knowledge. According to Miller, triperspectivalism "is a method whereby certain groups of *three* serve as comprehensive points of view."[24] In this book, we will be employing the specific theological method called triperspectivalism as understood by John Frame. Triperspectivalism has also been developed and articulated by an associate of Frame, Vern Poythress, in his work, *Symphonic Theology.*[25] Although Poythress represents a further development of triperspectivalism, he was a student of Frame and in order to stay on point, this book will limit the source content for understanding triperspectivalism to John Frame. For Frame, "triperspectivalism is, in the main, a pedagogical approach, a way of teaching the Bible— that is, doing what theology is supposed to do."[26] If triperspectivalism is a way of teaching the Bible so that it informs all of life, which is what Frame believes theology proper should be about, then it is closely related to the aims of CSF.

Triperspectivalism is a theological method which consists of three perspectives. Each perspective provides a way of viewing the truth and coming to a knowledge of the truth. As Esther Lightcap Meek states, "It is not appropriate to say that God *has* the truth, but rather, that he *is* the truth."[27] The three perspectives in triperspectivalism are referred to as normative, existential, and situational. Triperspectivalism builds upon the reality that all people see from vantage points in limited fashion. As Frame says, "A perspective, literally, is a position from which a person sees something."[28] And, triperspectivalism is helpful in theology.

Theology, for Frame, deals with applying the truth of God to all of life or as he says, "Theology is *the application of Scripture,*

---

24. Miller, *Triune God of Unity*, 32. Italics original.

25. Frame, "Primer on Perspectivalism."

26. Frame, *Theology in Three Dimensions*, xiv.

27. Meek, *Loving to Know*, 156.

28. Frame, *Theology in Three Dimensions*, 2.

by persons, to every area of life."[29] So, triperspectivalism is Frame's method for applying the truth of God to all of life. As an example of how this definition plays out with triperspectivalism, consider Frame at length:

> So I distinguish three perspectives of knowledge. In the "normative perspective," we ask the question, "what do God's norms direct us to believe?" In the "situational perspective," we ask, "what are the facts?" In the "existential perspective," we ask, "what belief is most satisfying to a believing heart?"[30]

Triperspectivalism viewed in this light is a method which does justice to his conviction that theology is applying the truth of God to all of life. It deals with how we respond to God's revelation which is our duty before God. As Frame states, "There are three main types of response we make to the revelation of God in the world: knowing, choosing, and feeling."[31] We can know God, choose God, and feel or experience God.[32] We can begin to see how these concepts are intimately connected to how we make disciples and form people.

Thinking of our interaction with God's world triperspectivally, there can be three main emphases. We can see God's control over the world and "his control provides a perspective ([Frame] calls it the *situational*) that sheds light on everything that happens."[33] Second, we can see God's authority in the moral universe. "Here we study the same universe as we studied from the situational perspective but with an emphasis of understanding our obligations."[34] This is what Frame calls the normative perspective. Third, we can study God's presence in the universe, which Frame refers to as the existential perspective. The existential perspective is that aspect

---

29. Frame, *Systematic Theology*, 8. Italics original.
30. Frame, "Primer on Perspectivalism."
31. Frame, *Theology in Three Dimensions*, 45.
32. Frame, *Theology in Three Dimensions*, 45.
33. Frame, *Theology in Three Dimensions*, 22. Italics original.
34. Frame, *Theology in Three Dimensions*, 23.

of knowledge and knowing which deals with the affections, emotions, and desires of people. Our existential experience is a type of knowing.

Joseph Torres summarizes triperspectivalism this way:

> There is always the person doing the knowing (the knowing subject), the thing being known (the object of knowledge), and the standard or criteria by which knowledge is attained. These three are interrelated such that each is a perspective on the whole knowing process. The first is the normative perspective, the second the situational perspective, and the third the existential perspective."[35]

Triperspectivalism thus represents Frame's epistemological framework (although it is not limited to epistemology as a tool). To recall, epistemology is a philosophical discipline that deals with how we come to know anything. Triperspectivalism deals with the ways in which knowledge is gained. Triperspectivalism argues that all three perspectives are coherent ways of engagement with knowledge.[36] "Every epistemic act has all three. The dimensions are distinguishable but never separable."[37] Knowledge in this sense is found in the fullness of God himself. And this experience of God is a gift, not something that we inherently own or possess as if God is our steward. Our experience and encounter with knowledge, being God himself, is derivative.[38] Our encounter with God is downstream of his revealing himself. Think of throwing three sieves in a river each with different filters. Whatever they catch would come downstream to them. In a similar way, our engagement with the knowledge of God comes more from a posture of receiving than scientific investigation. Michael Fourth puts it this way, "All knowledge is a reinterpretation of that which is already pre-interpreted and laden with

---

35. Torres, "Perspectives on Multiperspectivalism," 112.

36. Torres, "Perspectives on Multiperspectivalism," 106.

37. Meek, *Loving to Know*, 159.

38. Van Til, *Christian Theory of Knowledge*, 16. Referenced by Miller, *Triune God of Unity*, 75; Meek, *Loving to Know*, 157. Frame builds this off of Van Til's presuppositionalism to establish the source and basis of knowledge.

meaning by the Creator God."[39] We assume too much if we believe ourselves to be the primary meaning makers in our quest for knowing anything.

Taking Frame's understanding of the purpose of theology to be the application of God's truth to all of life, one can see how triperspectivalism is related to CSF. As stated previously, *CSF consists of approaches to spirituality that are distinctly rooted in the Christian faith and seek to form our material and immaterial capacities in their ability to connect with God and glorify him in life.* For Frame then, triperspectivalism can serve as a grid for CSF.

It is important to understand how Frame believes triperspectivalism to function in knowledge acquisition within formation. The way in which knowledge is gained will shape not only what kind of knowledge we discover but will also shape the way in which knowledge then transforms people. There is a relationship between knowing, knower, and action.

John Macmurray speaks of the relationship of knowing and action in this way:

> Any emodification of knowledge, since it is an agent's knowledge, necessarily involves a modification of his practical activity, whether this is intended or not. We clearly cannot change our ideas of the world in which we act without in some way modifying our way of acting. Even if we devote our lives to the pursuit of knowledge for its own sake, that is in itself a modification of our way of living.[40]

Macmurray's epistemological ponderings have profound implications in CSF. How we go about knowing will have a direct impact on how we live because we are agents of action not just thinking-things. Once we commit to knowing anything at all, that commitment then changes the trajectory of how we live.

I remember being stunned growing up that my parents knew the names of different types of trees in our yard. As a kid, a tree was

---

39. Fourth, "Christian Reflections on the Phenomenological Epistemology of Maurice Merleau-Ponty," 16.

40. Macmurray, *Self As Agent*, 185.

a tree. In my mind, there were Christmas trees that were always green and other trees that lost their leaves. Besides that, the idea of having a name for all of the "leaf-losing" trees was shocking to me. If you were to seek to know something about trees, you would begin to engage with literature regarding trees, and you would make choices regarding nature that would shape who you are. You would build a relationship with someone who knew how to distinguish between the types of trees. I might discuss with my relative who runs a nursery the differences between species of trees. You would begin to notice the types of trees in nature and the ability to notice the types would inform the type of person you become. The knowing would shape you.

Not only does triperspectivalism provide a Trinitarian foundation for knowledge acquisition, it also alleviates common tensions in CSF. Triperspectivalism can help negotiate and ameliorate the tensions between the material and immaterial in discipleship Noble argues that separating out reason and experience is not consistent with Scripture and instead argues that we should have "rational spiritual experience."[41] Our growth in Christ cannot be bifurcated into either knowledge (logic and reason) or experience but must incorporate both, which is consistent with a triperspectival view of CSF. Noble goes even further to say that our holiness should reflect the interpersonal love of the Trinity itself so that sanctification (or CSF) reflects the Trinity.[42] Both Noble and Macmurray are helpful in understanding triperspectivalism as a useful CSF tool because they both attack the dichotomous default that is so prevalent in twenty-first century American Evangelicalism. Meek is excellent in showing how the dichotomous default, wherein reason is reserved for "knowledge" and feeling for relationship, is self-destructive.[43] Separating two things that God designed to be utilized to know him creates malformed disciples.

With triperspectivalism, Frame does not divide topics into parts, as if each part were a completely distinct engagement with

41. Noble, *Holy Trinity*, 12.

42. Noble, *Holy Trinity*, 219–21.

43. Meek, *Loving to Know*, 139.

knowledge, but views topics from different perspectives. "Each of the three concepts is not an independent part, but a perspective on the whole."[44] This means that for Frame triperspectivalism is a method that is intended to provide a balanced engagement of the truth of God. It would be a mistake to think of triperspectivalism as a form of relativism or postmodernism (as will be explored later). Just as the Trinity cannot be broken into different parts without destroying the whole, so too with triperspectivalism it is important to recognize that each perspective affords a view of the truth without obscuring or trivializing the truth. Frame views each part of the whole as similar in relationship to the persons of the Trinity, as Miller shows in his figure "Epistemological Identity through Mutual Implication" (below).[45] Each perspective is considered knowledge, and yet each perspective does not totally represent knowledge on its own.

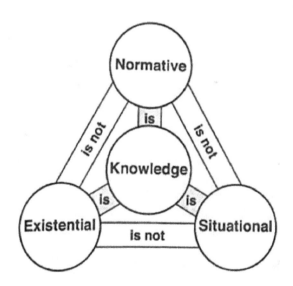

"Epistemological Identity through Mutual Implication"

---

44. Frame, *Systematic Theology*, 31.
45. Miller, *Triune God of Unity*, 279.

In order to better understand triperspectivalism as a theological method, the next few sections will unpack each perspective as Frame thinks of them. Triperspectivalism can be thought of as three lenses. Each lens has a particular way and understanding of encountering truth. Sometimes the lenses may complement one another and often they incorporate one another. They should never contradict one another. This concept of three lenses, in fact, is the illustration used on Frame and Poythress's website homepage to illustrate triperspectivalism.[46] These three lenses are the normative, the existential, and the situational.

NORMATIVE PERSPECTIVE

The normative perspective for John Frame is that perspective which sets out standards or norms. Frame defines the normative perspective as "a perspective of knowledge in which we focus on the world as a revelation of God's will."[47] This is not the only revelation of God's will, however. Norms or standards are those aspects of truth that are clearly set out to guide and establish boundaries. Think of reading a car manual or instructions for Ikea furniture (as deficient as they may be many times). These things are intended to be normative. For Frame, "The normative perspective is not the Bible; it is my understanding of the Bible in its relations to me and all creation . . . So understood, the normative perspective is certainly important, but it is not the Bible, and the primacy of Scripture does not of itself entail the primacy of the normative perspective."[48] "The Bible is also part of our situation . . . and of our experience."[49] To equate the normative with Scripture would be to minimize the authority of the word of God, relegating it to one category of knowledge.

The normative perspective deals with the "oughts" in the world. When looking at the world and seeking truth, we can understand that there are certain givens and ways that things work.

---

46. Frame, "Primer on Perspectivalism."
47. Frame, *Theology in Three Dimensions*, 28.
48. Frame, *Doctrine of the Knowledge of God*, 163.
49. Frame, "Primer on Perspectivalism."

It emphasizes the various "rules, laws, and norms for belief and action."[50] "Examples range from supposedly impersonal laws (laws of logic, planetary motion, gravity, etc.) to personal authorities (parents, employers, government officials, church leaders)."[51] The normative perspective deals with the basic language and definitions we employ to articulate the truth.

The normative perspective engages the Bible as God's revealed word such that we encounter the way things "ought" to be. Normativity is necessarily shaped by the other perspectives, but Frame does not allow the implied subjectivity of this reality to compromise his commitment to the conviction that the word of God is authoritative and inerrant. While we may misunderstand the Bible, the Bible as God's revelation is never wrong. Timothy Miller summarizes Frame's conclusion stating that "our understanding of Scripture can never be objectively certain."[52] This means that while the Bible is always true, our understanding of that truth is often skewed. Frame states that "our interpretation of Scripture will be fallible, subject to correction" and that this is inherently part of the process of knowing.[53]

With that said, Frame believes that "there is a hierarchy of norms, with Scripture as the highest" according to Joseph Torres.[54] In that sense, it could be said that Scripture is the norming norm for Frame: "When we seek to know anything, we must make special efforts to know ourselves and to restrain in ourselves those tendencies that suppress the truth rather than affirm it."[55] In this way, triperspectivalism seeks to simply acknowledge the effects of human sinfulness on our epistemological quest to encounter God.[56] But it is important to remember that "all knowing has three

---

50. Torres, "Perspectives on Multiperspectivalism," 113.

51. Torres, "Perspectives on Multiperspectivalism," 113.

52. Miller, *Triune God of Unity*, 85.

53. Frame, *History of Western Philosophy and Theology*, 722.

54. Torres, "Perspectives on Multiperspectivalism," 113.

55. Frame, *Theology in Three Dimensions*, 66.

56. Miller, *Triune God of Unity*, 46.

correlative aspects or perspectives: the existential, the normative, and the situational."[57]

According to Esther Lightcap Meek, the normative perspective includes "everything from our parents earliest wording of our world and our societally and historically shaped worldview, to the maxims of the expert or coach."[58] It is fundamental to our pursuit of knowledge because it shapes how we even perceive and process what is going on in the world around us when we "pick out some features of the world and not others."[59] Think of a child just learning to speak. In order to speak clearly at all, there must be some agreed upon language to which the child is exposed. This can be thought of as the normative perspective. The normative in summary is the perspective that deals with norms or standards.

EXISTENTIAL PERSPECTIVE

The existential perspective for John Frame is the perspective that deals with the emotions or affections in pursuing knowledge. It encompasses large parts of concepts related to desire and choice. Frame defines the existential perspective as "a perspective of human knowledge, focusing on our internal subjective experience in close proximity to God's presence."[60] In this way, the existential perspective is a more subjective understanding, but an understanding no less, of knowledge. While the normative perspective may be subjectively influenced in various ways, the existential perspective is more personally subjective in that it deals with personal emotions, desires, and affections which are oftentimes more obscure.

Frame ties the normative perspective to the existential perspective, postulating that "in one sense the process of knowing reduces to feelings—the sense that all my work has jelled into a meaningful shape. That jell is what gives me cogent understanding of all the

---

57. Meek, *Loving to Know*, 162.

58. Meek, *Loving to Know*, 79.

59. Meek, *Loving to Know*, 79.

60. Frame, *Theology in Three Dimensions*, 27.

facts, the arguments, the principles."[61] The existential perspective deals with the emotional engagement with truth rather than just a cognitive assessment as primarily represented by the normative. That is not to say that each perspective is void of the implications of the other. There is an overlap in which each perspective involves the others such that the existential still deals with cognition and the normative deals with emotions. The emphasis in triperspectivalism is not on the clear boundaries of the perspectives but instead on the unique focal points each perspective engages with knowledge. All knowledge will have an existential aspect.

While the normative perspective deals with the standards and norms of truth, the existential perspective deals with the affections of people. The way in which our affections are shaped and perceive truth does not change the truth but is helpful in discerning our relationship to the truth. "The *existential* perspective focuses on the person doing the knowing."[62] Or put another way, "we all bring spiritual dispositions, temperaments, biases, presuppositions, and memories to every act."[63] These preconditioned effects on our personality and perception affect the way we go about epistemology. From the Bible, we see that God is referred to as Father. The fact of that matter, the norm, is the normative perspective. The existential perspective is concerned with how we feel about that title for God based on our experience with earthly 'fathers.' As Frame states, "it is not enough to obey. We should obey for the right reason, from the right motive."[64] In this sense, the existential perspective begins to wrestle with the application of the normative to everyday life based on choice, motive, and desire. In thinking about formation, we should not just do the right thing and believe the right beliefs, but we should also behave and believe from the right motives. This moves us to the third perspective.

---

61. Frame, *Theology in Three Dimensions*, 69.
62. Torres, "Perspectives on Multiperspectivalism," 114.
63. Torres, "Perspectives on Multiperspectivalism."
64. Torres, "Perspectives on Multiperspectivalism," 72.

SITUATIONAL PERSPECTIVE

The situational perspective for John Frame is that perspective which deals with the experience of people in relation to the truth in the physical world. It is the context in which truth is worked out. Frame defines the situational perspective as "a perspective of knowledge in which we focus on the objects in the world."[65] The situational perspective has to do with the context of our obedience. When people engage the truth of God from a situational perspective, they are engaging truth within time, space, culture, family, church, and work. They are taking the oughts revealed in Scripture and practicing them in life situationally. The situational perspective finds a correlation in the philosophy of Michael Polanyi, as Esther Lightcap Meek points out, in the sense that "we live in the body as subsidiary; we do not experience it primarily as an object."[66] This Polanyian idea of body knowledge allows for knowledge to be perceived from our body and life experience, not just the acquisition of information. We are not just information receptacles that are given factoids about God. We are living people who live out our engagement with knowledge. For Meek,

> We can see the lived body feel of the subsidiary as the existential, and indeterminate future manifestations as the situational. We can see indwelling, for example, as practicing the existential in the situational.[67]

For Frame, this situational perspective provides the third and equally important way in which people can know God.

The situational perspective alone does not determine what the truth is, but instead points out the implications of knowledge in context. We can have situational knowledge. For example, God's command is to not bear false witness against your neighbor (Exod 20:16). This propositional declaration can be understood cognitively and existentially, but it also must be worked out situationally. The importance and application of not bearing false witness will

65. Frame, *Theology in Three Dimensions*, 28.

66. Meek, *Loving to Know*, 89.

67. Meek, *Loving to Know*, 169.

be understood differently by a child who is told not to lie to their parents than by someone on probation who has just been pulled over for speeding. The situation and context for obedience provide insight into the command itself. Think of the difference between explaining how to drive a stick-shift and actually driving a stick-shift. The latter is an example of the situational encounter of knowledge. The truth of God does not change, but one's understanding of it will change based on context. One's implementation of God's truth may be subjectively applied based on context. This is an important reality to remember in triperspectivalism, because each perspective is simply a different way of seeing the truth, but they alone do not justify the truth, nor do they become the truth in and of themselves.

While the normative perspective deals with the standards and norms of truth, the existential our emotions and affections in relation to truth (or the internal subjective personal understanding of the truth), the situational deals with the context and application of truth. In this sense, the situational perspective deals more with the external world. The situational invariably deals with issues in formation and discipleship related to relationships, obedience, and spiritual disciplines. Think of the ways that some churches have a liturgy in which people kneel during a time of confession. This is a situational experience wherein the act of confession is played out physically.

"The *situational* perspective directs us to the fact of human experience, including history, science, and evidences for our convictions."[68] The situational deals with the external world and how we process it. One can think of modernism and its pursuit of truth in terms of objectivity as the situational. There is a practical context and external world by which we can have knowledge at least in part. In many ways, the secular late modern world is a situational world where it is believed that all that can be known is only that which can be seen and measured. It is pragmatic in the sense that the knowledge that is most highly valued is that which is worked out in the material world.

So, what it is triperspectivalism? It is a teaching tool based in the Trinity which proposes that our encounter with knowledge

---

68. Torres, "Perspectives on Multiperspectivalism," 113.

comes from three focal points: the normative, the existential, and the situational. Triperspectivalism, when understood in such detail, can prove fruitful in summarizing tensions within other disciplines. For example, in the discipline of philosophy, triperspectivalism can be thought of with regard to three major schools of thought: the normative being rationalism, the existential being subjectivism, and the situational being empiricism.[69] Rather than force various schools of philosophical thought against one another, triperspectivalism provides balance.

In triperspectivalism, all three perspectives are essential and equal. They are equal in the sense that none are more significant than the others. They all serve important roles in dealing with knowledge and, consequently, formation. Triperspectivalism is a potentially valuable resource in CSF because it could help explain common tensions that oftentimes seem irreconcilable between the material and immaterial. Not only this, but it provides an approach to disciple making and formation which is not just pragmatic but also theologically grounded in God. This God glorifying approach could produce discipleship cultures that are more robust and durable than pragmatic programs that simply aim for knowledge transfer or obedience. What we have with triperspectivalism is a theological method that can create a paradigm of discipleship based on one of the most fundamental Christian doctrines, the Trinity. This paradigm of discipleship can help churches and people make disciples like Jesus wanted: disciples who learn to obey everything Jesus has taught us, disciples who do not just know what to obey, but obey and do so for the right reasons. It could create disciples who take into account not just what is right but how to apply what is right for the right reasons. It could create Christians who approach God's word with more humility in their understanding and application of it to all of life. But we're getting ahead of ourselves. This all sounds nice (if not a bit complicated) in theory. Before implementing this tool, it is important to consider some potential limitations and vulnerabilities of the model itself.

---

69. J. Anderson, "Presuppositionalism and Frame's Epistemology," 441.

CHAPTER 3

Triperspectivalism and Formation

THE BIKE CAME CRASHING down on top of me. I had been riding down trail 401 outside Crested Butte. This was my first time on this portion of the trail. I was spent and weak. I also did not fully comprehend some of the vulnerabilities of the bike. Because the brake cables were loose and the tread on my tires worn down, when I went to make a turn, the bike slid. I overcorrected and flipped over the handlebars. If I had taken a closer look at the bike before I hit the trail, I could have prevented this accident, which in the end thankfully only left me with a few scrapes. In a similar way, we need to inspect triperspectivalism for vulnerabilities that may not seem visible at first glance. While it seems to be an effective theological method that could enrich formation and disciple making efforts, it could have some liabilities. In order to examine those, we will consider substantial criticisms of triperspectivalism as a biblically faithful theological method.

Recall the potential strengths of triperspectivalism. It "challenges the approach to knowing that the defective default shapes."[1] Often the facts (the normative) are pitted against values (existential). With the help of triperspectivalism, both are held as important. Just consider how many people in our world view facts and feelings or experience

1. Meek, *Loving to Know*, 160.

as irreconcilable opposites. Triperspectivalism challenges this false dilemma. Fact is not the opposite of interpretation but is held in tension and together by interpretation. Instead of the normative being pitted against values and affections, the tension is maintained by a third polarity of epistemological discovery of truth in the situational. Truth does not become subjective, but instead better understood. As one discovers the norms and oughts of God, one then practices those norms and oughts. Those practices have a reciprocal dynamic in providing further knowledge of the implications of the norms and oughts. Not only this, but the existential is at all times present as we ourselves are agents of self in action, our affections and emotions inform our practices and *vice versa*.[2] David Clark points out that

> formation happens in a dialectic of experiences—in the moving back and forth between personal devotion to God and true community with fellow believers. Formation is less about specific theoretical beliefs.[3]

In this sense, triperspectivalism is formational.

Others have commented on the usefulness of triperspectivalism in understanding God's world, such as Pierce Hibbs, who argues that even if one has no salvific understanding or relationship to the triune God of the Bible, people are hardwired to perceive reality through stability, change, and context:

> Every human in history has relied on the static, dynamic, and relational perspectives of life, just as everyone has relied on the changeless plan of God the Father, the manifestation of the Son in human history, and the relational harmony between the Spirit and the Father and Son.[4]

Triperspectivalism can be a way that helps all humans better understand the ebbs and flows of life. From suffering to joy, triperspectivalism can be implemented in processing pain and happiness. In these ways, triperspectivalism is a helpful theological method for perceiving and analyzing human growth and development.

---

2. Macmurray, *Self As Agent*, 126.

3. Clark, *To Know and Love God*, 421.

4. Hibbs, "Do You See How I See?," 75.

Triperspectivalism can be an asset in CSF by assessing the individual seeking to grow, giving them a clear understanding of what God has revealed, and then providing real world application and practice. From a soul care and counseling perspective, Eric Johnson highlights the potential implications of Trinitarian thought for relational development. He says that

> Christians interested in the flourishing of human life (such as counselors) may legitimately formulate norms for human development and maturation based on the Trinity and develop corresponding criteria of personhood and community—informed by research and reflection on human life.[5]

Triperspectivalism, being grounded in the Trinity, would be an example of Johnson's suggestion in action.

Timothy Miller identifies four common critiques of triperspectivalism as a theological method that all fall under the charge of relativism.[6] For our purposes, we will highlight three of the four because they carry the heaviest charges. First, a common critique for triperspectivalism is that "if the 'knowledge of God's law, the world, and the self are interdependent and ultimately identical,' do we not risk elevating our feelings and understanding of the world on par with the authority of God's word?"[7] Put another way, by suggesting that there are three ways of knowing, does triperspectivalism promote relativism in that our feelings and experiences are on par with the normative? It would seem that triperspectivalism could compromise the authority of the Bible and God's revelation. Miller puts this concern succinctly, questioning, "If all of man's epistemological faculties are affected by depravity, how can he interpret revelation (even scriptural revelation) correctly?"[8] Tom Chantry suggests that triperspectivalism "makes the Word something other than

---

5. Johnson, *God & Soul Care*, 60.
6. Miller, *Triune God of Unity*, 77–78.
7. Torres, "Perspectives on Multiperspectivalism," 117.
8. Miller, *Triune God of Unity*, 87.

perspicuous. It may only be guessed at, never truly apprehended. That is the essential character of relativism."[9]

This critique was proffered by Mark Karlberg in 1989 when he accused Frame of taking the meaning of language out of the hands of God (Scripture) and situating the truth of God in human language instead.[10] According to Karlberg, "not only does Frame's method tend to undermine the authority of Scripture, but it challenges Scripture's attribute of perspicuity."[11] Perspicuity is the belief that one can come to a clear understanding of the text of Scripture through a plain reading of the text. This critique of triperspectivalism is valid if the attribute of perspicuity is understood in a very narrow manner developed from common sense realism. What if instead the scriptural attribute of perspicuity has been reduced to a representationalist or correspondence view of truth rather than understood holistically? Not that Scripture is less true, but that even for redeemed sinners our understanding of Scripture is still not perfect. The assumption that the perspicuity of Scripture means that everyone will interpret the Scripture the same way belies an approach to Scripture that is more scientific than relational. Not only this, but it is proven false by church history and the diversity of interpretations promulgated throughout time. When Scripture is treated the same as applied sciences, it becomes a problem to solve more than source of revelation pointing to the one who reveals.[12]

One needs to be clear that within triperspectivalism, the normative perspective is not the Bible itself. Triperspectivalism does not deny *Sola Scriptura*, "but instead is a methodological application of the hermeneutical circle."[13] Triperspectivalism puts in practice what is commonly known about Scripture, that there are hermeneutical challenges we face in approaching and discerning

9. Tom Chantry, "Confessional Redefinition and the Virtue of Honesty," quoted in Miller, *Triune God of Unity*, 87n22.

10. Karlberg, "On the Theological Correlation," 100.

11. Karlberg, "On the Theological Correlation," 102.

12. Don Payne, "Theological Method within the Canon" (lecture notes, Denver Seminary, February 21, 2018).

13. Torres, "Perspectives on Multiperspectivalism," 119; Frame, *Doctrine of the Knowledge*, 89.

the truth of Scripture. That is not to say that Scripture is unknowable, but instead that our knowing should always be held in check due to our limited understanding and sinfulness. Think of the last time you studied the Bible with someone else. I was recently discussing the context of Jesus's teaching on the Lord's Prayer regarding the concept of the Father rewarding us (Matt 6:6). My friend was trying to find correlative concepts of rewards in heaven in other New Testament verses. Another friend referenced her upbringing in the Greek Orthodox church with reference to crowns. By hearing their varied approaches to this one word that Jesus spoke, it did not diminish the truthfulness of what Jesus spoke but instead it brought to light the various ways each of us were limited and highly influenced in our approach to the Bible. Scripture is what "guides us epistemologically (telling us what truths we should embrace), ethically (building us up in holiness), and spiritually (feeding our hungry souls' need for divine fellowship)."[14] It is "the covenant document by which all other thought must be in subjection."[15] We do not get to operate as those who study Scripture, rather Scripture studies us and informs us as to where we are incorrect in our thinking.

Another critique proffered by some is that triperspectivalism is simply a mask for relativism. While the first critique was centered on the relationship of Scriptural authority within the method of triperspectivalism, this critique deals more broadly with the epistemological assumptions of triperspectivalism overall. Some have claimed triperspectivalism to be relativism in disguise. In Duane Smets's estimation, "If we accept triperspectivalism as an epistemology then we have inherently accepted postmodern relativism."[16] In Karlberg's estimation, triperspectivalism "amounts to theological confusion at a fundamental level."[17]

Let's look at this charge in more detail. For some, the potential of triperspectivalism to obscure the truth in various modalities

---

14. Torres, "Perspectives on Multiperspectivalism," 123.

15. Miller, *Triune God of Unity,* 88.

16. Smets, "Thinking Through Triperspectivalism."

17. Karlberg, "On the Theological Correlation," 103.

borders on relativism. Why? Because each perspective in triperspectivalism is equal, and, if each perspective is equal, is this not just another way to describe relativism? Furthermore, Smets claims "Jesus wanted his followers to solely look to God's Word as the source for truth rather than their personal experience or situational ethic."[18] This criticism reveals an assumption that there is objective knowledge without subjective influence. As Miller highlights, "The search for non-subjective truth is doomed from the start" because our status as creatures does not allow us to possess objective truth with the same degree of certainty as the originator and definition of truth, God himself.[19] While we may not have objective certainty because of this reality, "we can have subjective, personal assurance, knowing that God is sovereign over our every interpretation."[20]

Frame defends himself on this topic stating that "multiperspectivalism is not relativism. I am not saying that any viewpoint is a legitimate perspective. There is in ethics and in other disciplines an absolute right and wrong."[21] Frame argues that triperspectivalism "presupposes absolutism" in that "its metaphysical grounding is in the Trinitarian God who has revealed several aspects of his personal perspective to man."[22] In triperspectivalism, one is seeking to engage the ultimate knower of all perspectives. Frame "maintains that the three perspectives are equally ultimate, equally important. Each depends on the others, so that without the others, it could not be intelligible."[23] As Esther Lightcap Meek understands, "It doesn't matter where you 'start' on the triad."[24]

Simply because there are three perspectives on knowledge does not mean it is a relativistic pursuit. For Frame, triperspectivalism does not imply and should not be applied to mean that there are three parts of reality but instead three aspects from which to

18. Smets, "Thinking through Triperspectivalism," 4.

19. Miller, *Triune God of Unity*, 93.

20. Miller, *Triune God of Unity*, 94.

21. Frame, *Systematic Theology*, 1112.

22. Frame, "Primer on Perspectivalism"; Miller, *Triune God of Unity*, 84.

23. Frame, *Doctrine of the Knowledge of God*, 163.

24. Meek, *Loving to Know*, 162.

view reality.[25] Imagine you are hiking in the mountains of Colorado during the fall and you come upon an aspen grove. The leaves are a beautiful orange and red. You immediately notice the aspen grove with your eyes and take in their context amongst the dark green pines. You pull out your phone with a filter activated and you are able to see the aspens in a different manner, black and white, and this provides yet another way to appreciate and understand the aspens. Finally, you pull out some binoculars to get a closer look and you're able to see more clearly the individual trees and even the individual leaves. The three manners in which you have viewed the aspens do not change the aspens themselves. The aspens are just aspens. But there are simply three ways you have appreciated their beauty each multiplying your admiration.

What critics miss is that triperspectivalism does not lead to relativism, but that our relationship with God and knowing him is always rooted triperspectivally. As Torres points out,

> instead of denying that truth is "out there" to be discovered, perspectivalism recognizes that our epistemic access to this truth is relative to the particularities of our gifts, nationality, gender, chronological location, etc.[26]

For many Christians and those who seek God, it has been presupposed that knowledge is simply a matter of right versus wrong. There is truth and not truth. We are either wrong or right. What triperspectivalism helps us understand is that the truth is out there, but how we ascertain the truth is much more than a simple formula or rational deduction. Rather than triperspectivalism promoting some kind of theological pluralism where multiple contradictory positions could be true, it "is ultimately the outworking of a chastened objectivism."[27] Meek believes that "capable and effective knowing requires intentional (not necessarily explicit) employment" of multiple perspectives.[28] She argues that "the major and operative anchor of any act of knowing is tacit (not articulated or

25. Frame, *Theology in Three Dimensions*, 25.

26. Torres, "Perspectives on Multiperspectivalism," 113.

27. Torres, "Perspectives on Multiperspectivalism," 117.

28. Meek, *Loving to Know*, 83.

explicit)."[29] Miller explains that those looking for an uninfluenced and non-contextual objective view of Scripture and truth are deceiving themselves.[30] According to Miller, Frame

> denies that there is any non-subjective truth waiting to be known behind personal and contextual factors. The primary reason to deny such *truth* is because God's knowledge is not objective (i.e., non-subjective). God is an absolute person, and as such, his knowledge is exhaustively *personal*.[31]

Because God is personal, knowledge is not something outside of him but is essential to him and as such is essentially personal. God does not submit himself to some standard of objective truth outside of himself. He himself is the truth. Myron Penner asserts that

> postmodernists are not advocating sheer relativism when they assert the perspectival character of human thinking and access to truth, nor are they abandoning all normativity or relegating all perspectives to the same meaningless status.[32]

In fact, perspectives on knowledge have less to do with the object of knowledge than the knower themselves. This is also asserted by theologians such as Kevin Vanhoozer, who writes that right worship of God is not just about objective truth as understood to mean facts about God: "Worship concerns objective truth *and* our right relation to the truth."[33] Vanhoozer references the philosophy of Kant to show that he "believed that knowledge necessarily involved both ideas and experience."[34] Our knowledge, our experience, and our affections shape our understanding of truth. They do not change the truth. James K. A. Smith himself concurs, stating that

---

29. Meek, *Loving to Know*, 93.

30. Miller, *Triune God of Unity*, 88.

31. Cornelius Van Til, *A Survey of Christian Epistemology*, quoted in Miller, *Triune God of Unity*, 88–89. Italics original.

32. Penner, "Cartesian Anxiety," 98.

33. Vanhoozer, "Worship at the Well," 11.

34. Vanhoozer, "Worship at the Well."

"Recognizing the social and communal conditions of knowledge—that our knowledge is *relative* to our social context—does not entail that everything is just 'made up.'"[35] Frame finds it unfortunate that perspectivalism as a name is associated with triperspectivalism because, as he explains, the concept of perspectivism has been associated with philosophers such as Nietzsche or Charles Sanders Peirce who are explicitly relativistic.[36] This has led to a great deal of confusion and many of Frame's critics simply misunderstand how he defines triperspectivalism.

A third and final critique of triperspectivalism to be considered here has to do with the authority it retains as a theological method since it is not explicitly stated in Scripture. Should not the authority of triperspectivalism be questioned if it is not biblical or found in the Bible? Because it is a theological construct, is not its authority diminished?[37] While triperspectivalism is a theological construct and method, Frame develops it using theological conclusions from Scripture: "It is simply false to suppose that constructs are mutually exclusive with accurate teaching."[38] That is, it is false to suppose that constructs and accurate teaching are incompatible. If this were true, then we would have no word for the Trinity on which triperspectivalism is based.

JUSTIFICATION FOR THE USE OF TRIPERSPECTIVALISM AS A THEOLOGICAL LENS FOR ANALYSIS

Now that we have examined some of the common critiques of triperspectivalism, we need to make the case that triperspectivalism is not just a legitimate and useful theological method, but that it can be used as a tool to analyze other theologies. We may have

35. Smith, *Who's Afraid of Relativism?*, 87.

36. Frame, "Primer on Perspectivalism." Perspectivism and perspectivalism are not synonymous although Frame treats them as such in this context. Perspectivism as a philosophical discipline is more commonly associated with relativism.

37. Torres, "Perspectives on Multiperspectivalism," 119. Torres raises this issue rhetorically.

38. Torres, "Perspectives on Multiperspectivalism," 119.

a legitimate tool in triperspectivalism, but can the tool be utilized to study other systems of thought? Specifically, can triperspectivalism be used as a philosophy of CSF? First, we need to consolidate what we have discussed and provide some final verification that triperspectivalism is conversant with CSF. John Frame summarizes triperspectivalism in this way:

> Human knowledge can be understood in three ways: as knowledge of God's norm, as knowledge of the situation, and as knowledge of ourselves. None can be achieved without the others. Each includes the others.[39]

Looking at this definition of triperspectivalism through the lens of CSF, one can see that triperspectivalism provides a simple and helpful way to articulate the complexities involved in CSF. As previously stated, *CSF deals with approaches to spirituality that are distinctly rooted in the Christian faith and seek to form our material and immaterial capacities in their ability to connect with God and glorify him in life.* Triperspectivalism allows for the situational cultivation of practices that are contextually sensitive and appropriate. And it highlights the importance of knowing oneself so that our material and immaterial capacities are dealt with appropriately.

Triperspectivalism rejects relativism, the idea that all positions are equally legitimate, in favor of absolutism. Triperspectivalism is similar in nature to a philosophy of learning or Christian education. As Doug Blomberg points out, "Scriptures orient us to an understanding of persons as integral rather than dualistic beings."[40] As people develop and grow, multiple capacities are at play. Overly relying on a rationalistic encounter with the truth will lead to a malformed and incompletely educated person. As Johnson points out, "A merely intellectual relationship with God, based solely on conscious head knowledge . . . is not enough to heal the unconscious regions of the soul."[41]

For Frame, triperspectivalism is a helpful tool in the life of a Christian. As he summarizes,

39. Frame, *Doctrine of the Knowledge of God*, 75.
40. Blomberg, "Heart Has Reasons," 62.
41. Johnson, *God and Soul Care*, 66.

> These aspects of the Christian life are perspectival in the sense that we obey God's commands (normative) only when we apply them to the whole world (situational) from the heart (existential). Insofar as we fail to make these applications from the heart, we have not obeyed God's norms.[42]

Triperspectivalism has obvious implications for CSF based on Frame's understanding of the method. Far from diminishing the truth of God, it in fact heightens the demand of God's way in the lives of people. People can falsely believe that failing to live in step with God's will, or what is commonly called sin, deals with one of three things: behavior or thought or affections. But triperspectivalism shows that our sin can be in all three perspectives at once.

In using triperspectivalism as a theological lens, it is important that Frame himself "maintains that the perspectives are equally ultimate, equally important, and equally mutually dependent: each needs the other two to be what it itself is."[43] As Timothy Miller states, "Triperspectivalism can be described as a method where distinct elements cohere in perfect harmony."[44] In differentiating it from general perspectivalism, triperspectivalism "argues for *three* distinct focal points from which knowledge can be viewed."[45] There is no primary way to engage knowledge, but instead all three are equally valid.

In relation to CSF, triperspectivalism from Frame's perspective is a useful tool. Frame, however, does not advocate a certain method or philosophy of spiritual formation from triperspectivalism. In fact, Frame himself admits that he is "not a specialist in the doctrine of sanctification or in the disciplines of what is now called 'spiritual formation.'"[46] Instead he proposes three methods for growing in sanctification: "the Word, fellowship, and prayer."[47]

---

42. Frame, *Theology in Three Dimensions*, 75.
43. Meek, *Loving to Know*, 162.
44. Miller, *Triune God of Unity*, 106.
45. Miller, *Triune God of Unity*.
46. Frame, *Doctrine of the Christian Life*, 911.
47. Frame, *Doctrine of the Christian Life*, 918.

"First, God has provided us with a norm or standard to tell us what is right what is wrong."[48] That norm would be the word of God. It is to be a "guide to believers."[49] The second way in which people can grow in holiness, according to Frame, "is by reminding us of what God has done for our salvation" as we gather in fellowship with others.[50] It is God's deliverance of his people that is to be the motivation for obedience.[51] This would be the situational. The third manner in which people can grow in sanctification according to Frame is through prayer, which for him is the existential perspective. With all of this established, what would it look like to take seriously Frame's triperspectivalism and attempt to apply it to spiritual formation? While he himself admits that he is not a specialist in spiritual formation, what could it look like to take his model and use it within discipleship and spiritual formation? To that task we turn to next.

CONSTRUCTING A TRIAD FOR CSF

While John Frame has not developed a triad for CSF or discipleship, his method is simple to develop into such a triad. The method is intended to be utilized constructively and creatively. Frame has developed over one hundred triads and Timothy Miller has summarized some boundaries for constructing triadic relationships based on the works of Frame and Poythress.[52] This will be very important to understand because it will lay out clear guidelines an boundaries to the subsequent spiritual formation triad we attempt to construct. Imagine you are trying to design a new house. If you were not aware of the necessary components of what makes a house a house (e.g., foundation, walls, roof), you would probably create "not a house." We want to create a CSF triad based on

48. Frame, *Systematic Theology*, 989.

49. Frame, *Systematic Theology*, 990.

50. Frame, *Systematic Theology*.

51. Frame, *Systematic Theology*.

52. Miller, *Triune God of Unity*, 232.

triperspectivalism rather than "not a triad." To do that, we need to understand what constitutes a legitimate triad in triperspectivalism.

First, "when something original is reflected in a secondary entity and the two are inseparably associated (based on God's persons)," it could be a triad.[53] This means that a triad could be discerned if it is based on the Trinity and the coinherence of the relationships therein. The Father, Son, and Spirit have a relationship of mutual indwelling (or perichoresis). There is a connectedness to the persons of the Trinity. If two things are distinct and yet reflect the perichoretic relationship of the Trinity such that they are intricately connected as well, a triadic relationship could be described. While perichoresis does not automatically indicate three-ness, it does provide an indicator of the possibly of three-ness. All of this to say, a principle in developing triads deals with the relationship and inter-connectedness of the topics involved. A dog and cat share a close relationship in that they are both animals that are common household pets. A dog and a car share a distant relationship for obvious reasons. There is a coinherence of correspondence to dog and cat while there is not with dog and car.

The second criteria, according to Miller, for formulating a triad concerns the decrees of God "where beginning moves to accomplishment and then to application consummation (based on God's eternal decree)."[54] In this sense, the triadic relationship must be related to the order of God's decrees in terms of the eternal plan, accomplishment, and application of redemption in some way. The three must relate to one another in the sense that they all reflect a common purpose and theme together. The three aspects of the triad need to have a common *telos* or purpose. They do not necessarily need to reflect a soteriological theme as much as reflect a similar commonality of theme. The concepts should have a similar scope of application. Attempting to construct a triad from the purposes of football to the implementation of those purposes in pharmaceuticals would be unintelligible. However, attempting to construct

---

53. Miller, *Triune God of Unity*, 232.
54. Miller, *Triune God of Unity*.

a triad from the purposes of football to youth development have more teleological interplay.

Third, "where there are significant analogies to the lordship attributes or the three perspectives that emerge out of them (based on God's character)," it could be described as Trinitarian and triadic.[55] According to this third boundary, the Lordship attributes of the Trinity should be reflected in the triad (control, authority, and presence). There should be in each of the perspectives a common representative for the normative, existential, and situational perspectives.

Using the previous definition of CSF (*CSF consists of approaches to spirituality that are distinctly rooted in the Christian faith and seek to form our material and immaterial capacities in their ability to connect with God and glorify him in life*), we can simplify and enhance it using triperspectivalism. CSF consists of approaches to spirituality that are distinctly rooted in the Christian faith and seek to form our *head, heart, and hands*. This triad has been suggested in Christian education literature but without a connection to Frame.[56] It has also been suggested by James K. A. Smith, who states that "It's not only our minds that God redeems, but the *whole* person: head, heart, hands."[57] Alternatively, because head, heart, and hands are easily misconstrued, we could say that triperspectival CSF seeks to form our *duty, doctrine, and devotion*. As Gary Parrett and Steve Kang state, "A faithful ministry of the Gospel will attend both to the essence of the Gospel and its implications for doctrine, devotion, and duty."[58] In this triad, duty, doctrine, and devotion replace the concept of material and immaterial capacities and the *telos* of connecting with God and glorifying him in life.

---

55. Miller, *Triune God of Unity*, 232.

56. Parrett and Kang, *Teaching the Faith*, 117. "Those who have been engaged in ministries of Christian education and formation will recognize the value of the pattern emerging from Scripture and affirmed through church history. Educators have long recognized a similar triad of "head, heart, and hands." In formal language: three domains of learning are acknowledged: cognitive, affective and behavioral (or psychomotor)." Estep and Kim, *Christian Formation*, 136.

57. Smith, *You Are What You Love*, 9.

58. Parrett and Kang, *Teaching the Faith*, 105.

These three words would have the following relationship to triperspectivalism. Duty would be equivalent to the situational, or how we are to live in this life. It encompasses our potential outworking, context, and application in CSF. Doctrine is equivalent to the normative, or what we are to believe. Devotion is equivalent to the existential, or affections, desires, and emotions. This triad fulfills the three boundaries and principles for constructing triads and shows promise for transferability and implementation in discipleship and formation theories. The simplification of CSF into this triad also honors the pedagogical design of triperspectivalism in that it creates a useful teaching tool. By using this simple definition built of formation and discipleship, which is developed from Trinitarian theology, we have the advantage of our philosophy of ministry not just being pragmatic but deeply theological.

So, what's next? Now, we will take this new triad for a test run by using it to analyze the CSF and discipleship concepts proposed by James K. A. Smith. Imagine triperspectivalism to be a car brand, such as Toyota, and this proposal (duty, doctrine, devotion) a new car offered by that brand. It just so happens that this new car is intended to tackle one of the most fundamental commandments from God, which is to make disciples (Matt 28:19), making it a potentially important contribution to this task and also to the outworking of triperspectivalism. But before we can take the car off the lot, we need to pick a trail to explore to test its capabilities. The trail I would like to explore would be the formational and discipleship theories of James K. A. Smith. Why don't we map out what that trail looks like?

CHAPTER 4

James K. A. Smith's Theology of Spiritual Formation

ONE OF THE FIRST discipleship relationships I led was painful. I was newly ordained and in the throes of seminary life. Discipleship for me had felt like a moving target and had historically looked more like mentoring. So, when it came time for me to begin to disciple others as a pastor, I was determined to try something different. Why? Because I was only a few years older than the man I was discipling. It felt like I did not have enough life experience to disciple someone. What made the relationship painful was that I was trying to exert more cognitive weight than my friend was prepared to handle. I remember saying to him, "Part of me discipling you will involve me telling you what to believe." Now to be sure, discipling others involves helping them in their beliefs. However, reducing discipleship to cognitive assent is relationally troublesome, to say the least. It essentially amounts to a "believe what I believe" version of discipleship. This approach for me was not born out of a vacuum, however. It was informed by an Evangelical culture that typically practices a reductionistic discipleship approach in which cognitive belief is the champion. This is part of what makes James K. A. Smith's counter-theories to formation so appealing.

James K. A. Smith's Theology of Spiritual Formation

In order to test out triperspectivalism, we need to find a formidable theory of formation to challenge. At this point, we have a nice theory (or at least I think it is nice). But we need to actually put it to work against current methods and philosophies being employed in churches today. This chapter will provide an overview of James K. A. Smith's understanding of CSF so that an assessment can be performed using triperspectivalism. Think of this chapter as mapping the path that we anticipate taking our triad down. We want to make sure that the path we take is the correct one and makes sense for our equipment. Smith's understanding of CSF was summarized in a brief manner in chapter 1. However, this chapter will provide a more robust explanation. In particular, it will highlight his convictions regarding formation and specific criticisms of the Reformed Evangelical world with respect to formation.

While Smith's work as a philosopher covers a variety of topics, his work in his *Cultural Liturgies* series and *You Are What You Love* make his case most strongly for his particular brand of CSF. The aim of Smith's project is formation and discipleship. He states that

> the genesis of the project was a desire to communicate to students (and faculty) a vision of what authentic, integral Christian learning looks like, emphasizing how learning is connected to worship and how, together, these constitute practices of formation and discipleship.[1]

For Smith, "Christian formation is about proper and intentional teaching and training of the body and its habits, not just imparting correct doctrine."[2] Smith believes much of the Evangelical tradition has been most concerned with imparting correct doctrine. This is best exemplified by those promoting worldview studies and analysis. Before diving into Smith's positions and justifications for those positions on CSF, it is important to revisit his relevant work to this topic to ensure a proper understanding. We want to take Smith on his own terms.

---

1. Smith, *Desiring the Kingdom*, 11.
2. Anderson, "Imagining the Kingdom," 188.

JAMES K. A. SMITH'S SCOPE OF WORK ON CSF

It can be challenging to transpose philosophy into formation. While Smith's background is in philosophical theology, continental philosophy of religion, and philosophy of the social sciences, his most recent work has involved taking this philosophical background and applying it to Christian formation.[3] As William Peterson states, Smith's most recent work is "a phenomenological analysis of religious practice."[4] That is, it is a study and deconstruction of Evangelical formation theory.

Smith builds on his philosophy background to create a proposed system of education for the Christian life and Christian institutions in his *Cultural Liturgies* series. This series is the most appropriate for analysis when it comes to Smith's understanding of CSF. In the three books comprising the series, he deconstructs and then reconstructs a vision for Christian institutions embracing his understanding of how people and cultures grow in godliness. Much of his proposal builds on postmodern philosophy wedded with Christianity. However, it must be cautioned that Smith's understanding of postmodernism does not stem from a popularized relativistic subjectivism. This will be discussed in more detail below. His positions are highly nuanced and require careful analysis. As he often states, he would like to plunder the Egyptians with regard to postmodern thought and philosophy so as to enhance our own understanding of Christianity.

In *You Are What You Love*, Smith summarizes much of the philosophical thought he fleshes out in his *Cultural Liturgies* series. Think of it as the cliff notes version. The main thrust of this book is that our affections drive what we know. In this sense, he applies a pragmatic understanding of language and truth to Christian formation in general. For Smith, what we do (our actions) shapes what we desire, which shapes what we believe. The social community of faith where we find ourselves defines for us what the truth is through how we practice the truth. As opposed to correspondence or representationalist claims to truth, Smith believes a pragmatic

---

3. Smith, *Curriculum Vitae*.

4. Peterson, "Imagining the Kingdom," 733.

understanding, or what he calls relativism, best accounts for our encounter with truth.[5] Within a representationalist approach to truth, truth is understood to have a one-to-one relationship with our understanding. We are believed to have a complete ability to understand truth. If I say blue, we would all agree on what exactly blue means. For Smith, our approach to truth is much more nuanced so that blue is perceived to mean a variety of things to different people. For example, when I say blue, I imagine the Kansas City Royals color. But you may have in mind a different shade. With that in mind, he believes that people encounter God and grow in godliness more through community practices than objective or propositional truth claims.

This relativistic view is critiqued by Douglas Groothuis who claims that a "defense of propositional revelation has always been a central tenet of Evangelicalism and primary plank in the debate over biblical inerrancy."[6] For Groothuis, a correspondence or representationalist understanding of truth is essential to Christianity. However, Smith holds George Lindbeck in high regard with respect to the epistemological assumptions of relativism and their implications for ecclesiology and mission, as has been mentioned previously. According to Groothuis,

> Lindbeck stresses that doctrine has a regulative function in various communities that is not directly (if at all) propositional. If so, doctrinal "truths" only apply within the community; they cannot successfully or normatively refer to a reality outside of the community.[7]

This means that truth is only relevant to those people within a community as they have defined it. The question essentially boils down to how we discover truth and the authoritative nature of that truth. Is truth merely relativistic and defined fundamentally by a community of faith, or is truth defined by revelation?

5. Smith, *Who's Afraid of Relativism?* This work describes Smith's case that relativism is useful and should be embraced.

6. Groothuis, "Postmodernist Challenge to Theology," 5.

7. Groothuis, "Postmodernist Challenge to Theology," 10.

Smith views Lindbeck as an example of how relativism or pragmatism can be successfully employed doctrinally and ecclesiologically. However, according to Groothuis, "Theology ought to be derived from Scripture, not community and experience, although these will always shape our theologies in various ways."[8] Groothuis represents his position well but perhaps too readily dismisses the two other ways how people encounter the truth, hence why triperspectivalism is a helpful way to summarize the epistemological encounter (and eventual growth) with God. Because John Frame believes that all three perspectives are equally authoritative epistemologically and their unique interconnectedness makes them useful and valid, he and Groothuis, while similar, have fundamentally different epistemological methods.

JAMES K. A. SMITH'S EMPHASIS ON SPIRITUAL FORMATION

With those things established, it is time to focus more specifically on Smith's understanding of CSF. Smith's work deals with sanctification, discipleship, and CSF. He believes that

> Our sanctification—the process of becoming holy and Christlike—is more like a Weight Watchers program than listening to a book on tape. If sanctification is tantamount to closing the gap between what I know and what I do . . . it means changing what I want.[9]

Read that again and you may be picking up on a triad that Smith unknowingly alludes to. What do I know? What do I do? What do I want? Smith believes that change comes from practice that cultivates a different desire. Changing one's affections does not begin with intellectual transformation because intellectual transformation is not where we begin to develop as people, according to Smith.

Todd Pickett clarifies, "If it is not entirely clear from the title, James K. A. Smith's new book [*You Are What You Love*] is about

---

8. Groothuis, "Postmodernist Challenge to Theology," 10.

9. Smith, *You Are What You Love*, 65.

discipleship."[10] Discipleship and CSF go hand in hand very often. As Smith writes,

> Discipleship and formation are less about erecting an edifice of Christian knowledge than they are a matter of developing a Christian know-how that intuitively "understands" the world in the light of the fullness of the gospel.[11]

While CSF may not be the central outworking of Smith's efforts, there is no doubt that his work has direct implications for how he believes people change and grow.

In the view of David Morlan, Smith claims that a poor Evangelical anthropology and application of that anthropology in discipleship "leaves Christians unformed and vulnerable to being unwittingly seduced by counterfeit kingdoms."[12] For Smith, this is due to thinking of people as thinking-things, meaning empty containers needing knowledge in order to change. He instead proposes that humans are higher animals that are still driven in many ways like animals, by instinct.

JAMES K. A. SMITH'S PROPOSED PRIMACY OF THE "GUT" IN SPIRITUAL FORMATION

Smith argues that what is most important in our spiritual transformation is not our ability to believe but instead to imagine what the kingdom is like.[13] It is our affections and desires which are fundamental in CSF for Smith. This imagining happens through liturgies or processes by which we are reoriented towards what is true, good, and right. Elsewhere, Smith argues that church renewal "hinges on an understanding of human beings as 'liturgical animals,' creatures who can't *not* worship and who are fundamentally formed by worship practices."[14] In other words, we are hardwired to

---

10. Pickett, "You Are What You Love," 304.
11. Smith, *Desiring the Kingdom*, 68.
12. Morlan, "Review," 1.
13. Smith, *You Are What You Love*, 93.
14. Smith, *Imagining the Kingdom*, 3.

be worshipping creatures. What forms us are worship practices that orient us to the gospel. The practices are community-based practices rooted in tradition that give us the know-how to believe the gospel at all. Before believing the claims of Christianity, we become accustomed to and desire Christianity because of the context in which we find ourselves. We also, as Smith convincingly argues, are drawn to alternative visions of the good life that are not Christian. These are what Smith refers to as secular liturgies.

When Smith speaks of this concept of being driven by affections or being liturgical animals who operate based on instinct more than reason, he suggests that we should think of the word "gut." What Smith means by gut is that

> we make our way in the world by means of under-the-radar intuition and attunement, a kind of know-how that we carry in our bones. As lovers—as desiring creatures and liturgical animals—our primary orientation to the world is visceral, not cerebral.[15]

This idea, that people are driven by desire and love in our intuition, has a rich history in Christianity leading back to Augustine. According to Smith, this is counter to what most modern Reformed Evangelicals believe about our orientation to the world. Most, he claims, at least practice formation that is primarily cerebral, represented frequently in the realm of apologetics and worldview formation.

Smith proposes that rather than human beings being thinking-things, they are instead feeling-things. "In this alternative model of the human person, the center of gravity of our identity is located in the heart—the visceral region of our longings and desires, the gut-level region of the *kardia*."[16] Our identity does not come from what we believe but instead what we desire. True knowledge, according to Smith, is not based upon facts but instead upon desire and a "know-how."[17] This is reaffirmed as a pragmatic argument in

---

15. Smith, *You Are What You Love*, 33.

16. Smith, *You Are What You Love*, 14.

17. Smith, *Desiring the Kingdom*, 67.

his book, *Who's Afraid of Relativism?*, where Smith affirms that our knowledge is "based on prior know-how."[18]

In this sense, what is most important in the formation of people is that they are shaped in their capacities not with more facts and worldview but instead with cultivated desire through liturgy. This is not far off from Polanyi, who speaks of "tacit knowledge" as represented by Esther Lightcap Meek.[19] In Meek's understanding of Polanyi, our prior knowledge and lived knowledge has a far more significant impact on our quest for knowledge than commonly accepted. However, Smith's claim is more exclusivise in that he believes cultivated desire through liturgy to have not just an impact, as in Meek and Polanyi, but to be the foundational way in which we come to a knowledge of the truth. It is the starting point of formation.

Smith does not argue simply that worship is sufficient for education, but that it is primary.[20] Worship, or liturgy, is the primary way in which we come to desire and know the truth at all. There is no doubt about this in his writings. Even though Smith disputes that he denigrates worldview into a secondary tier of importance, there can be no doubt that much of his writing on formation places the priority with the cultivation of desire through practice. The paradigm of change for Smith seems to be in order: body, then heart, then mind. Smith even defensively predicts this observation early on his book, *Desiring the Kingdom*, where he states that he

> is not advocating a new form of pious dichotomy that would force us to choose between either the heart or the mind. Rather [he] will sketch an account of the priority of affectivity that undergirds and makes possible the work of the intellect. In short, [he's] not arguing that we love, and therefore we need not know; rather, we love *in order* to know.[21]

Smith believes that we are creatures who love so that we can know. Our affectivity is what drives our intellect.

18. Smith, *Who's Afraid of Relativism?*, 123.

19. Meek, *Loving to Know*, 85.

20. Smith, "Two Cheers for Worldview," 55–58.

21. Smith, *Desiring the Kingdom*, 17–18.

He builds much of his argument on Maurice Merleau-Ponty's epistemic philosophy of the living body. This is the idea that our knowing is based in our body and our practices. Think of how you know how to ride a bike. Your body learns it, and you can remember it. This is connected to human development theory wherein children learn how to go about life in the world relationally before they are even aware they are learning a way of being.[22] When a child is learning vocabulary and concepts, it is done through teaching the child the use of things and words, not just facts about the world. It makes me think of when my children were younger, and my wife and I would teach them numbers and letters. The best way to teach them is to put it into practice. "There are two goldfish." "There are four apples." Before explaining the etymology of the word apple and describing its place within the plant world, we simply show them an apple.

HISTORICAL PROBLEMS WITH CHRISTIAN FORMATION ACCORDING TO JAMES K. A. SMITH

James K. A. Smith observes several deficiencies regarding contemporary CSF in Evangelical churches. His main grievance with much of the discipleship happening within the Evangelical world is that the focus is on information rather than transformation. He summarizes this common approach in this way:

> If we assume that human beings are thinking things who are always "on," who think through every action and make a conscious decision before ever doing anything, then discipleship will focus on changing how we think. Our primary goal will be informing the intellect so that it can direct our behavior.[23]

Smith views this as insufficient. It is interesting is that much of cognitive behavioral therapy makes use of this same method. By talking

---

22. Plass and Cofield, *Relational Soul*, 48.
23. Smith, *You Are What You Love*, 33.

out our problems and discovering new beliefs, we can change our behaviors.

Smith believes that CSF should not spend as much energy on changing how we think. As he states, "Discipleship is more a matter of r*eformation* than of acquiring *in*formation."[24] As Tawa Anderson points out, "Smith insists that worldview is inadequate and insufficient for proper Christian formation."[25] Morlan concurs with Anderson's summary, claiming Smith "makes a highly intellectual case that the church should quit aiming for the intellect in discipleship."[26] This is not to say that Morlan endorses Smith's perspective but that Smith's perspective is commonly agreed upon by at least Morlan and Anderson.

For Smith, all of this means that

> our most fundamental orientation to the world—the longings and desires that orient us toward some version of the good life—is shaped and configured by imitation and practice. This has important implications for how we approach Christian formation and discipleship.[27]

If the foundational way we approach the world is shaped by imitation and practice, then it would change how we go about formation and discipleship. He argues that "we can't calibrate the heart from the top down, through merely informational measures. The orientation of the heart happens from the bottom up, through the formation of our habits of desire."[28] Practice and liturgy are what shape our desires. In this understanding, discipleship would be first and foremost concerned with practice and liturgy.

"Smith objects to an overemphasis on rationality and correct ideas that he feels are a part of the Reformed model of Christian worldview education."[29] This model, according to Smith, is guilty of placing too much focus on the intellect and having right ideas.

24. Smith, *You Are What You Love*, 19.

25. Anderson, "Imagining the Kingdom," 190.

26. Morlan, "Review," 2.

27. Smith, *You Are What You Love*, 19.

28. Smith, *You Are What You Love*, 25.

29. Thiessen, "Educating Our Desires," 48.

Because the Reformed Evangelical tradition is committed to the inerrancy of Scripture, formation can often become more about facts over and against experience and affections. Smith situates these problems mainly in the Reformed Evangelical camp because that is the camp within which he resides. Because of this overemphasis, many Christians have been co-opted by competing allegiances because they are unequipped and have not had their desires cultivated for Christlikeness. They have not been paying attention to what is really driving their spiritual life. We have been so busy checking the instrument panel, we have not looked up to see what direction we're driving.

Not only does Smith object to the primacy of rationality in formation, but he also postulates that we are formed by our behaviors and practices even before our rational conclusions. As Morlan summarizes, "Smith's project reminds us that, like it or not, we are indeed shaped by what we do."[30] We are pre-loaded with interpretations of Scripture before we even approach Scripture. Our desires and affections have been shaped by our embodied state. In fact, God designed it this way. When we pretend that our history and story do not shape our ideas about God and the Bible, we undermine our ability to connect with God and love others. It is detrimental to our understanding of God's truth to believe that our behavior does not affect our understanding of that truth. We are constantly being shaped by our environments to perceive truth in a certain manner.

Smith's argument for this (the idea that our behaviors and environment inform our desires and subsequent understanding of truth) is laid out most clearly in *Desiring the Kingdom*. First, he argues that "Human persons are intentional creatures whose fundamental way of 'intending' the world is love or desire."[31] This of course is in contrast to viewing the fundamental way of "intending" the world to be through cognition. Second, he argues that "This love or desire—which is unconscious or noncognitive—is always aimed at some kind of vision of the good life."[32] That is to say, our

30. Morlan, "Review," 4.

31. Smith, *Desiring the Kingdom*, 62.

32. Smith, *Desiring the Kingdom*, 63.

love and desires are teleologically oriented to make us pursue what we believe to be the greatest good. Desires are shaped by the purposes that we have been shown to be good in life. Third, "What primes us to be so oriented . . . is a set of habits or dispositions that are formed in us through affective, bodily means, especially bodily practices, routines, or rituals that grab hold of our heart through our imagination, which is closely linked to our bodily senses."[33] These bodily practices and habits are what inform and set the stage for our vision of the good life. Our desire is shaped by vision, and our vision by liturgy.

JAMES K. A. SMITH'S RELATIONSHIP OF DESIRE AND ANTHROPOLOGY

James K. A. Smith asks, "What if the center and seat of the human person is not found in the heady regions of the intellect but in the gut-level regions of the heart?"[34] As Petersen summarizes regarding Smith's anthropology, "The thesis is advanced that human beings are not primarily thinking or believing beings, but only secondarily so. What is first is desire."[35] Elsewhere Smith posits his question in this manner, "What if, instead of starting from the assumption that human beings are thinking things, we started from the conviction that human beings are first and foremost *lovers*?"[36] He seeks to highlight the significance and primacy of desire in formation. He suggests that in terms of human composition, the intellect follows the heart. We are liturgical animals driven by instinct and desire.

This comes from the conviction that "We are primarily *desiring* creatures rather than *intellectual* creatures."[37] The gut is "the lower precognitive emotional center of the person."[38] This gut is the primary way our interpretive and formational progress is directed.

33. Smith, *Desiring the Kingdom,* 63.
34. Smith, *You Are What You Love,* 7.
35. Peterson, "*Desiring the Kingdom,*" 774.
36. Smith, *You Are What You Love,* 7.
37. Peterson, "Imagining the Kingdom," 733.
38. Morlan, "Review," 2.

It is equivalent to desire. Our formational direction is not so much determined by what we believe intellectually but instead by what we desire in our gut or lower precognitive emotional center. It is this area, the gut, which Smith believes is most fundamental in CSF.

Smith states that "what counts as 'rational,' then, *depends* on the rules and norms of a discursive community. Concepts are *relative to* a community of practice."[39] For Smith, "A pragmatist account of meaning and knowledge does not preclude referential claims; it just accounts for those claims differently."[40] Smith believes that "this pragmatist account amounts to a philosophical appreciation of our creaturehood, an appreciation of the contingency that characterizes creatures."[41] For him, a correspondence theory of truth presumes to possess a godlike status that does not take into consideration our sinfulness and limitations. His understanding of a representationalist or correspondence theory of truth creates a picture closely resembling a fundamentalist approach to truth.

So, this is Smith's take on formation. This has been important because we do not want to put words in his mouth. We want to have a very clear picture of what the lay of the land is if we are going to apply our triad. Let's summarize. In this chapter, we have sought to accurately represent Smith's understanding of CSF. Smith's work is saturated with a concern for the formation of people. He believes that formation must reprioritize the role of affectivity in formation over pure intellect. Not only this, but community practices and liturgy are what shape affections and desires. Smith proposes that the Reformed Evangelical world lacks an accurate understanding of formation and instead settles for worldview analysis and acquiring information. Alternatively, he believes that we must capture the desires of people by giving them a vision of the good life through Christian liturgy. Because we want to establish that the triad of doctrine, devotion, and duty is a legitimate tool for spiritual formation, we need to test it out. Now that we established a solid test case, let's see how they converse.

39. Smith, *Who's Afraid of Relativism?*, 141.
40. Smith, *Who's Afraid of Relativism?*, 166.
41. Smith, *Who's Afraid of Relativism?*, 170.

CHAPTER 5

Putting Triperspectivalism to Work

BEHIND THE CABIN WAS a place that proved a formidable obstacle course for any vehicle. I had recently sold my truck and replaced it with a smaller truck that was designed and built to go off-road. It had a locking rear differential. There were different settings for snow, mud, and sand. It had different modes for rock crawling. And I wanted to see how it worked. We took it to this "road" with a steep grade, some creek crossings, and rock obstacles to put it through the paces. I discovered new noises, new features, and that the chrome exhaust pipe tip would probably have to go after it got bent on a rock. By taking the truck on a path that was formidable, I was able to discover its capabilities and limits. In a similar way, Smith's thinking has proved to be a force with regard to spiritual formation and discipleship. We want to take triperspectivalism on this path to test out its capabilities and limits. Strap in, because it may get a little bumpy. This chapter will employ the triad previously constructed (duty, doctrine, devotion), however we will retain Frame's language of normative, situational, and existential so as to be clear and consistent. We've been preparing for this chapter up until this point so do not quit now. This is about to get interesting. How does Smith's theory of formation stack up against triperspectivalism?

Smith desires that we "reconsider the relationship between practice and belief."[1] In this sense, using Frame's triperspectivalism to assess Smith's propositions regarding CSF is in line with Smith's aim in his own project. One of the challenges of this endeavor is to find equivalent concepts and definitions in order to accurately assess the concepts of formation in Smith's thinking through the grid of Frame's triperspectivalism. For example, it is important to consider if Frame and Smith are using the word *belief* in the same way. In order to solve this problem, an initial summary of Smith's perspective will be presented with a working definition of Frame's understanding of that perspective. This will be followed by possible correlations in Smith's work, after which an analysis will be done. If we are able to successfully analyze, both appreciatively and yet critically, Smith's philosophy of CSF using Frame's triperspectivalism, then two things will be made clear. First, Frame's triperspectivalism could reasonably be employed to analyze other philosophies of CSF. Secondly, it could stand alone as a philosophy of CSF and discipleship.

NORMATIVE PERSPECTIVE IN ANALYSIS

The normative perspective consists of the rules and standards of knowledge. It is important to note that Frame argues that "Scripture neither teaches nor implies the 'primacy of the intellect,' but speaks of either fidelity or infidelity in the person as a whole."[2] That is, Scripture speaks to faithfulness with what we have more than the achievement of some intellectual prestige as a benchmark of formation. The normative perspective is that perspective of truth which deals with standards and norms. Think of the mathematical equation $2 + 2 = 4$. This is a norm or standard. When examining the truthfulness and validity of any claim to knowledge, the normative perspective provides us with the boundaries and obligations delivered. The cognitive realm of reason and its delineated boundaries logically form some of the substance of the normative perspective.

1. Smith, *Desiring the Kingdom*, 133.
2. Powlison, "Frame's Ethics," 761.

While Frame argues that each perspective is equally effective at understanding the truth at least in part, Smith argues that this normative perspective is not the way in which truth is to be sought in a transformational way. This is a significant difference between Frame and Smith. Smith denies that liberation and formation can come through cognitive understanding at least as a starting point. He does not give even the possibility of priority to cognitive understanding and in doing so shows that he does not view perspectives as equals. There is not a scenario in which cognitive understanding, or the normative perspective, could be a first step towards transformation for Smith.

According to Smith, "To question thinking-thingism is not the same as rejecting thinking."[3] He goes on to say, "You won't be liberated from *de*formation by new *in*formation. God doesn't deliver us from the deformative habit-forming power of tactile rival liturgies by merely giving us a book."[4] The Bible for Smith, as with other forms of propositional truth, tends not to be able to deliver us from rival visions of kingdoms. This is because, our engagement with the Bible is typically a propositional endeavor according to him. He does not deny the importance of the normative, but in his philosophy of CSF and discipleship, it is greatly diminished and reprioritized. It would be a mistake to think that Smith does not believe cognitive engagement to be important. He simply views it as derivative of cultivated desire. Thoughts are downstream of desires. Consider how you pick out what to wear each day. Smith would argue that your choice was less of a rational decision and more of a reflection of what we desire in life. My desire to wear black and grey is more reflective of who I want to be than who I think I am. It is not even that I could articulate who I want to be, it is just in my gut.

Smith's opinions of a normative engagement with the truth would be equivalent to his convictions regarding propositional truth. It may be useful—and at times necessary—but it is not the entry point for transformation. In fact, for Smith, the normative perspective yields to the situational and existential. He may not

3. Smith, *You Are What You Love*, 6.
4. Smith, *You Are What You Love*, 83.

believe this is the only way for transformation, but he does make the case that it is the best and the primary way. Because Smith views oughts, norms, standards, and general correspondence theories of truth with suspicion, the normative perspective in his theory of CSF is seen as a suspicious and unreliable means by which to be formed.

In summary, when looking at Smith's philosophy of formation through the lens of the normative perspective (or doctrine, to use our triad), it is clear that the "oughts" and norms are defined by the community of faith and are in service of practice. The normative perspective shows that Smith's CSF does not place a high value on the quest for knowledge intellectually in terms of priority. Instead, the normative perspective is downstream of both the situational and the existential perspectives. If there is an order in Smith's concept, which it seems there is, then the normative would be the last stop.

EXISTENTIAL PERSPECTIVE IN ANALYSIS

What is the role of desire and affection in CSF? For Frame, desire and affection are part of what constitutes his existential perspective (or devotion, in our triad). The existential for Frame is simply another focal point by which people can come to a knowledge of Jesus Christ. Frame even goes so far as to say that "Your knowledge begins with feelings within your body."[5] For Frame, knowledge or truth may be first acquired by feelings within your body. This existential perspective consists of emotions, affections, and desires. These are constitutive of the existential focal point of epistemic discovery. We can know things and grow in knowledge from our emotions and desires.

For Smith, affections, or the existential perspective, is the center point of CSF. It is the cultivation of desires and affections that is the main thrust of his philosophy of CSF. Love is instructive in the sense that it points us in the direction of what we are going to know in the normative sense. Desire and love position us to know anything at all, according to Smith. This does not match Frame's

5. Frame, *Theology in Three Dimensions*, 65.

commitment that the existential perspective is simply another avenue to discover truth because, for Smith, it is the primary avenue to discover truth. There is a linear manner in which people discover truth, according to Smith.

In Smith's understanding, the existential perspective would be that which we know but cannot yet articulate as knowledge. It is precognitive knowledge. Think of how you know how to drive a car or how you know your mother loves you. It is not just the words spoken or the acts performed, it is a deep sense of being loved. "The most basic way that we intend the world is on the affective order of love."[6] Further down on the same page, Smith claims, "This orientation is something that comes before thinking; thus we've described it as precognitive."[7] However, for Smith, this precognitive "knowing" is formed by the third and final perspective: the situational, which will be addressed in the next section.

Smith claims, "In some ways, we belong *in order* to believe."[8] By this, Smith claims that a sense of belonging directs our believing. This would seem to contradict the priority he places on desire. Instead of desire being primary, belonging to a people is primary. Belonging as a concept is more at home in the situational aspect, wherein we are found within a local community of faith that shapes our understanding of truth before we can express the truth propositionally. This corresponds with Smith's commitment to "language as use" and concepts being defined relative to a community of practice, as previously mentioned. For Smith, the community shapes the epistemological journey and trajectory for Christian formation. Belonging directs the course of believing.

SITUATIONAL PERSPECTIVE IN ANALYSIS

The situational perspective has to do with context in place and time relationally. As John Frame states, "To know anything, you need

---

6. Smith, *Desiring the Kingdom*, 80.

7. Smith, *Desiring the Kingdom*, 80.

8. Smith, *You Are What You Love*, 81.

to understand that you yourself are part of the story."[9] It has to do with the external world. While the existential focused more on the immaterial, affective person, the situational focuses more on the material. James K. A. Smith claims that "the way to the heart is through the body," by which he means the external context we find ourselves in and the way in which we interact with that context.[10] Elaborating on this perspective elsewhere, Smith says, "The way to the heart is through the body, and the way into the body is through story."[11] For Smith, the situational perspective drives the existential.

It is the normative (transformational knowledge, not just facts) that is acquired through the existential perspective (using Frame's language), which is shaped by the situational (using Frame's language). You might need to read that again because it is key. Let me restate it for us. Smith believes that what I do shapes what I want, which in turn shapes what I think. As stated previously, Smith believes that formation comes from practice (or what he calls liturgy), which cultivates a different desire. However, if affections are formally downstream from practice, then how does Smith justify the implementation of practice at all affectively? How would one change their desires if they did not desire to change in the first place? If in order to change desires, a new liturgy must be implemented, whence does this desire for a liturgy arise? It seems that one must be predisposed to practice in order to gain affections. For example, if one were to be involved in religious practices that were not Christian, it would seem impossible for them to be transformed other than to adopt Christian practices first. This almost leads to a deterministic theory of formation where we are pre-determined to particular desires based on context. What would be the impetus for liturgical formation, if the desire for liturgical formation only happens subsequent to liturgical formation? Put another way, if the only way one can cultivate rightly ordered desires is through different liturgies, how would one gain the desire for this different liturgy in the first place? I like Texas A&M football. A lot. In Smith's

9. Frame, *Theology in Three Dimensions*, 65.

10. Smith, *You Are What You Love*, 85.

11. Smith, *Imagining the Kingdom*, 14.

approach, if you wanted me to like another team, you would need to immerse me in that culture first and foremost. You would need to take me to Austin, Texas, and watch the college team there play football, and then I would develop affections for them. But why would I want to do this in the first place? I do not like that team. Not only this, but the normative perspective in this regard is seemingly absent and unnecessary for Smith.

Smith straddles the situational and existential perspectives by claiming, "The practices of Christian worship function as the altar of Christian formation, the heart and soul, the center of gravity of the task of discipleship."[12] Seen through the lens of triperspectivalism, Smith's vision for formation seems truncated and absent of some very essential realities for formation with respect to the normative perspective; for example, intellectual development through teaching, reading, preaching, etc.

Smith places something at the center of discipleship which is simply one aspect of it when examined triperspectivally. While he argues that churches should embrace their role in the formation of people by being great at liturgical practices that steep people in the Christian story, he overplays his hand to the detriment of the normative perspective and, inadvertently, the existential. According to Smith, "In our outward-oriented zeal to translate the faith into 'relevant' messages for a post-Christian culture, we have only eviscerated the community of *practice* necessary to sustain witness to the risen Christ."[13] In other words, what maintains and cultivates our experience with the risen Christ is the community of practice. Stephen Turley proposes, "The key term for Smith's educational proposal is practice: the core of practice centers on the fact that bodily actions and habits are fundamental to shaping and molding our desires."[14] Contrary to many Evangelical theologies of CSF, behavior shapes belief. There can be no doubt that the situational perspective is the primary means for transformational knowledge

12. Smith, *Desiring the Kingdom,* 213.

13. Smith, *Who's Afraid of Relativism?*, 178.

14. Turley, "Practicing the Kingdom," 132.

for Smith. It is the entry point of liturgy that is the primary and most important means of formation.

As Tawa Anderson points out, "Smith argues that an accurate anthropology embraces our embodiment and rejects mind-body dichotomies."[15] In this sense, Smith and Frame agree that a core reality of formation must involve our embodied situation. However, it seems that Smith is compartmentalizing the person and setting the compartments up in a linear fashion, much like a modernist. For example, Smith makes his argument in this way:

> It's not that we start with beliefs and doctrine and then come up with worship practices that properly "express" these (cognitive) beliefs; rather, we begin with worship, and articulated beliefs bubble up from there.[16]

The historic legitimacy of this claim is suspect ecclesiologically. The church has traditionally allowed its worship to be informed by its rich biblio-theological heritage. What Smith claims would be the equivalent of attempting to start a sport with a ball and making up the norms and standards along the way. This linear thinking in terms of development and formation goes against his relativistic convictions (where in relativism things are in flux). It seems he is approaching CSF from the modernist position wherein there is a strict order to formation. His approach would be enhanced by a triperspectivalism because it would both correct some common problems in his CSF and yet maintain an openhandedness regarding the linearity of formation. This would offer Smith a more holistic and integrated approach.

Frame would argue that it is a false dilemma to choose between the existential and the situational. Triperspectivalism solves this tension for Smith. Esther Lightcap Meek believes that "Frame proposes this approach . . . because it is superior to any attempt to make the one perspective prior to the other or induce a truncated, sequential linearity."[17] There are in fact three ways to encounter truth, none of which are primary or necessitate a starting

15. Anderson, "Imagining the Kingdom," 188.

16. Smith, *Desiring the Kingdom*, 70.

17. Meek, *Loving to Know*, 160.

point.[18] The normative, existential, and situational for Frame can all be starting points by which we begin to encounter the truth of God. None of them alone are sufficient for understanding God's truth. In triperspectivalism, CSF requires that all three perspectives be present in order to understand more fully and grow in God's truth. Smith, in his work, has "emphasized that humans are first and fundamentally affective creatures shaped by practices . . . "[19] Smith clearly believes that the preeminent approach to God's truth must begin with the situational perspective when examined from a triperspectival approach to CSF. But we're getting ahead of ourselves. We need to at least acknowledge where these two great thinkers agree. Let's look at some flat spots in the road.

AREAS OF AGREEMENT

Propositional truth alone is incomplete the spiritual formation of people. On this, James K. A. Smith and John Frame agree. "It's not only our minds that God redeems, but the *whole* person: head, heart, hands."[20] Frame would reply to this proposition with "Amen." Smith believes that worldview alone does not equip people to be renewed in their capacities. Worldview might give people the right answers but does not guarantee godly affections. Frame would agree with this sentiment and add that affections and community practices exclusively are also insufficient for formation of the whole persons. Instead, he would propose that the normative, existential, and situational components of formation must all come into play. For Frame, worldview as Smith understands it would fit under the normative category. Both Smith and Frame agree that that the situational and existential perspectives are important.

18. Frame, *Doctrine of the Knowledge of God,* 162–163; Miller, *Triune God of Unity,* 279. This belief in the lack of order within a triperspectival theological method is solidly what Frame believes but Timothy Miller, in his work, argues that the order within the Trinity necessitates a procession within triperspectivalism whereby the normative is the first. It is Miller's conviction that this preserves the authority of Scripture and honors the method's Trinitarian basis.

19. Smith, *Desiring the Kingdom,* 134.

20. Smith, *You Are What You Love,* 9.

Smith and Frame both agree that the truth must be worked out in context. Frame tends to see eye to eye with Smith in that it is not possible to have "purely objective" knowledge; that is, knowledge devoid of our own experiences, thoughts, or concerns. Instead, what we need is not purely objective knowledge, but an encounter with God who entered our creaturehood in the person of Jesus Christ. "He identifies himself in and through our thoughts, ideas, and experiences."[21] Smith expresses as one of his greatest concerns in Christian education and formation is that we have lost our creatureliness and sense of contingency. Triperspectivalism provides a helpful antidote. Triperspectivalism provides a way to acknowledge our creaturehood and contingency before the face of God.[22] How? By acknowledging the reality that our knowledge is only in part compared to the knowledge of God, we start from a place of humility in our formation. Through the incarnate Christ, we realize that encountering God is not just about encountering a set of propositional truth claims; it is about encountering a personal spiritual being. And this triune God comes to us as Father, Son, and Spirit.

Frame's triperspectival approach to knowing "directly challenges the theory-practice dichotomy of the default mode. Traditionally, we think that theory is what matters, and theory must precede practice."[23] For many Christians, knowing is simply having the ability to retain facts, but as Frame and Smith point out, knowing is much more than that. Knowing is not simply fact retention and articulation. It is a holistic endeavor involving our head, heart, and hands. A major emphasis, as Eric Johnson points out with reference to therapy, in formation "involves learning how to know, worship, and love God in his diverse perfections."[24]

Esther Lightcap Meek highlights that the opposite of this would be obedience preceding knowledge (something Smith seems to embrace). Christianity, for many people, consists of knowing rightly in order to live rightly. But as Meek proposes, it is not that

21. Frame, *Doctrine of the Knowledge of God*, 65.

22. Miller, *Triune God of Unity*, 276.

23. Meek, *Loving to Know*, 179.

24. Johnson, *God and Soul Care*, 180.

simple. "We already do place knowledge in the context of trust; we just haven't been allowed by the prevailing paradigm to see and accredit it."[25] Meek builds a bridge between Smith and Frame by showing that knowing is a dynamic experience that is not just about learning facts (as if learning facts was a one-dimensional activity). Instead learning, or knowing, involves a dynamic experience within a triadic discovery of God.

Smith and Frame both agree that affections must play a significant role in CSF. Frame seems to hint at some of Smith's concepts in stating that the past events of salvation "have changed our hearts, so that today our dispositions are entirely different."[26] These dispositions are matters of the heart and our desires. This inner change for Frame "is correlative to the indwelling of the Holy Spirit in the believer."[27] The Holy Spirit indwells the believer at conversion and thus produces new affections and desires. Smith believes these desires for God are given to us by the Holy Spirit.[28] The existential for both Frame and Smith play a significant role in CSF.

Smith and Frame both pull from Ludwig Wittgenstein to tease out their respective positions on issues of language and meaning.[29] This is an interesting overlap because while they disagree in some key areas, they pull from some of the same waters. For Smith, Wittgenstein provides a helpful criticism of realism and representationalism in language.[30] Wittgenstein proposes that language and meaning have more to do with use rather than with representationalism and meaning tied to objects.[31] Think of how we understand the word *run*. There is a dictionary definition of *run*—to go faster than a walk. In fact, this would have been the common definition throughout much of history. But today if someone says, "I like to run," it is assumed they are referring to the exercise and practice

25. Meek, *Loving to Know,* 179.

26. Frame, *Systematic Theology,* 992.

27. Frame, *Systematic Theology,* 992.

28. Smith, *You Are What You Love,* 10.

29. Wittgenstein, *Preliminary*; Frame, *Systematic Theology,* 363. Smith, *Who's Afraid of Relativism?,* 41.

30. Smith, *Who's Afraid of Relativism?,* 40.

31. Frame, *History of Western Philosophy,* 489.

of running and not simply the basic activity of going faster than a walk. Our understanding of the word is shaped and even changes by the way it is used.

Smith believes this to be a helpful and necessary critique of a modern understanding of language that is based much more on realism and correspondence theories of truth. Wittgenstein provides an emphasis on contingency and creaturehood that reframes our quest for understanding with a sense of humility in light of God's sovereignty. In Smith's understanding, this is contrary to the common quest for truth and understanding that is more analytic and based on a representationalist view of language. This, for Smith, is represented in worldview and propositional truth as the primary means of formation. Based on Wittgenstein, language and definitions become defined in terms of use in community.[32] Smith builds his philosophy of CSF from this belief.

For Frame, his definition of theology reveals his philosophical borrowing from Wittgenstein as well. He believes theology is best done when applied to life. Theology is a "meaning in use" activity. Frame believes that "*meaning* is best employed to designate that *use* of language that is authorized by God."[33] However, Frame clarifies, "We must say that the meaning of an expression is its *God-ordained* use."[34] So, while Frame may pull from relativistic or pragmatic thinkers, he does not do so to the extent that Smith does in developing the basis of his theological method.

AREAS OF DISAGREEMENT

Here we arrive at the tension where we explore the differences between Frame's triperspectivalism and Smith's theories of formation. Frame would likely disagree with Smith with regard to the relevance and transferability of propositional truth. Smith seems to propose subjectivism insofar as he "urges the hearer to bring his worldview

---

32. Smith, *Who's Afraid of Relativism?*, 72.

33. Frame, *Doctrine of the Knowledge of God*, 33.

34. Frame, *Doctrine of the Knowledge of God*, 97.

into line with his own deepest beliefs and feelings."[35] With respect to human knowledge, Frame divides "the created world into three objectives of knowledge that are perspectivally related to one another and that correspond to our three lordship attributes."[36] Triperspectivalism for Frame provides a holistic account for knowledge.

This is relevant in relation to Smith because he discusses at length what it means to truly know something. The three objects of knowledge for Frame are: *self, world,* and *divine revelation.*[37]

> *Divine revelation* represents God's authority as the norm that determines the truth or falsity of what we claim to know. *World* is the situation into which God has placed us, the whole course of nature and history under his control. *Self* is the knowing subject, existing in personal intimacy with God as present to his covenant people.[38]

If we use this triad to analyze Smith's theories, then we see they quickly come into conflict. Smith argues that knowledge must start with our embodied ritual and practice, or the world. Frame counters to say that knowledge is not only about us and our situation but also about Divine revelation. As Doug Blomberg points out:

> Though we should not go as far as psychologist Jonathan Haidt (2001), who suggests that we are emotional dogs with rational tails—for this would be but to reverse rather than to transcend the traditional prioritizing of human functions—we can accept this further affirmation from "social intuitionism" (or "moral foundations theory") that emotions do play a vital role in learning. In place of the Western exaltation of an abstracted intellect, we should advocate a bodily epistemology and pedagogy, respecting the physiological-emotional mind that neuroscience, significant strands of philosophical reflection, and the Jewish and Christian Scriptures, affirm.[39]

35. Frame, *Theology in Three Dimensions,* 77.
36. Frame, *Systematic Theology,* 719.
37. Frame, *Systematic Theology,* 719.
38. Frame, *Systematic Theology,* 719.
39. Blomberg, "Heart Has Reasons," 64.

This is to say that learning and transformation is a holistic endeavor that is not honored by creating simplistic dichotomies regarding the fundamental priority of points of access to transformational knowledge. This seems to be exactly what Smith proposes, a dichotomy regarding the fundamental priority of points of access to transformational knowledge.

Esther Lightcap Meek argues that body knowledge is essential to our discovery of truth and growth in our knowledge of truth.[40] Much of Smith's argument is built on the epistemic philosophy of Merleau-Ponty called the lived body. Now stay with me. I realize that this section is pulling together a lot of seemingly random twentieth-century philosophy. However, in order to appreciate the differences between Frame and Smith, it is essential to unpack the philosophies which inform their perspectives.

Merleau-Ponty developed a phenomenological approach to epistemology to show that language and meaning is shaped by our embodied nature and context. Smith uses both this and Merleau-Ponty's understanding of the pre-reflective and pre-theoretical to argue that our knowledge of God is based more in cultivated desire through practiced liturgy than the import of worldview.[41] Meek shows that while this is an important perspective in epistemic discovery, it is not the only or paramount form of discovery and subsequent formation.[42] Our body knowledge must be held in relation to the normative and situational perspectives in order to craft a well-balanced epistemology and understanding of formation. Without a grounding of the lived body, truth becomes situationally and contextually defined. Using Frame's language, the truth becomes entirely defined by and subject to the situational perspective.

This highlights a major vulnerability with Smith's work. He seems to reverse the priority rather than transcend them with his liturgical formation. Blomberg articulates this problem when he says that

40. Meek, *Loving to Know*, 107.

41. Fourth, "Christian Reflections"; Smith, *Imagining the Kingdom*, 41–46. Fourth summarizes Merleau-Ponty in his article. Smith makes this case extensively in his work *Imagining the Kingdom* by using Merleau-Ponty as a source for his own convictions.

42. Meek, *Loving to Know*, 77.

just as it is a mistake to identify this core with cognitive or intellectual functioning, so I also take it that it would be wrong to equate the heart with the affective domain, over against the cognitive. This latter notion, common in the opposition of "heart" and "head," naturally promotes anti-intellectualism, not an inclusive conception embracing cognition and affect.[43]

And yet, this is what Smith seems to put forward as a better way of CSF.

In speaking of the importance of the Bible in spiritual growth or formation, Frame highlights, "We need to run the Bible passages through our minds over and over again, until we take it to heart."[44] This seems to run against Smith's proposition that in order to cultivate the heart, we must be oriented properly in liturgical expressions that capture our vision and desires for God's ways. Smith asks, "What if education weren't first and foremost about what we *know* but about what we *love*?"[45] Education for Smith becomes a concern regarding liturgy and affection above propositional knowledge. As Noble displays, "The basic idea is the Platonist one that we are drawn to what we love. We cannot be human without being drawn to what we love and every human being is therefore motived by love."[46]

The aforementioned rhetorical question posed by Smith betrays the underlying reality that in order to love we must have acquired a certain disclosure of knowledge about the object of our loving. How is one to practice CSF without even a limited commitment to a correspondence theory of truth wherein definitions and words reflect their reality? In order to love something, we must know it cognitively or normatively in some respect. Of course, this knowing must involve desire and interpersonal relationship, but to diminish the importance of facts and norms is detrimental to knowing at all. Not only this, but Christian liturgy assumes that the formational aspect of preaching and teaching is not simply

---

43. Blomberg, "Heart Has Reasons," 66.
44. Frame, *Systematic Theology*, 1050.
45. Smith, *You Are What You Love*, 138.
46. Noble, *Holy Trinity*, 60.

propositional but transformational. Preaching and teaching Scripture is not simply the articulation of neutral information. It is a means through which God acts salvifically (Rom 10:14–17).

Michael Fourth points out this weakness in Merleau-Ponty's thinking stating, "It merely describes the manner in which knowing does occur rather than why it occurs."[47] Knowledge and love should not be bifurcated to create a false dilemma of priority. If I were to claim to love my wife who has brown hair and blue eyes but described her with green eyes and blonde hair, could I really claim to love her?[48] Theissen asks, "Why can't we inhabit the world as both thinking and affective creatures?"[49] Frame would take it further to ask: Why can we not inhabit the world as thinking, affective, and situational creatures? Or as David Clark points out:

> Some may find God through a worldview-oriented grid for encountering reality, and others may find God as a character in a narrative-oriented grid. We should not prejudge that the worldview grid—an abstract, propositional way of coming to knowledge of God, of encountering truth of God—is superior to a concrete, narrative, or more vividly experiential way.[50]

Theissen, disputing Smith's claims about priority, states, "We must be very careful whenever we suggest that one thing comes before another or that one thing is more important than another."[51] Theissen suggests that worship and worldview should be combined. Smith argues, "Some of our action is directed by conscious deliberation and reflection on our beliefs," but he does not believe they are primary.[52] Smith's arguments would be greatly served by trip-

47. Fourth, "Christian Reflections," 18.

48. Assuming of course that she did not recently balayage her hair. However, that would still not change the reality that her hair is brown even if temporarily blonde in some way.

49. Theissen, "Educating Our Desires," 52. It could be argued that inhabitance incorporates the situational in which case Theissen is making a triperspectival assertion without knowing it.

50. Clark, *To Know and Love God*, 233.

51. Theissen, "Educating Our Desires," 49.

52. Smith, "Two Cheers for Worldview," 56.

erspectivalism to avoid these issues of "chicken or the egg." Why can't some people encounter transformation through conscious deliberation and others through practice? While Smith himself denies that he proposes a dichotomous split between worship and worldview (as shown previously in his response to Theissen), it seems he would be greatly helped by using triperspectivalism to round out his philosophy of CSF.[53] Rather than being accused of creating yet another modernist rendition of linear priority in formation, he could show a more balanced approach by using triperspectivalism.

In Smith's proposal for CSF, he attempts to navigate the tension between determinism and human autonomy. In issues of formation, we must seek to participate with God in formation while rejecting a deterministic, naturalistic worldview. However, "While Smith seeks admirably to maintain the balance between the two poles of rational autonomy and mechanical determinism, he too often leans to the deterministic side."[54] Smith at least implies, if not states outright, that our formation is determined by the situational perspective within which God has placed us.

Smith seems to prioritize the subjective aspects of salvation over and against more objective aspects. Frame does not believe that objective and subjective aspects of human experiences of God should be separated.[55] For Frame, the objective aspects of salvation are "aligned with what [he] has called the situational perspective . . . and the 'subjective' [are] the existential perspective."[56] He is worth quoting at length here to make his point:

> But these cannot be separated. The situational perspective is a world that includes my inner life, and I understand objective facts by means of my inner ability to know. At the same time, the existential perspective is obtained by its factual environment. My inner ability to know comes about through factors outside myself: my parents, my education, my experience, and especially God.[57]

53. Smith, "Two Cheers for Worldview," 56.
54. Anderson, "Imaging the Kingdom," 189.
55. Frame, *Theology in Three Dimensions*, 36.
56. Frame, *Theology in Three Dimensions*, 36.
57. Frame, *Theology in Three Dimensions*, 36.

The strength in triperspectivalism is its commitment to objective truth without giving into fundamentalism.

Smith operates from a pragmatic relativist point of view, recognizing some of the limitations of that epistemological tradition but nevertheless employing it widely in both *You Are What You Love* and *Cultural Liturgies*. His understanding of CSF is grounded in pragmatic relativism, such that the practices that form people serve as the starting point for our understanding of the truth. They not only serve as the starting point, but also the determiner of what truth is because truth is determined by the practices of that community. In his theory of formation, there seems to be no problem with relativism as long as it is defined in such a way so as to not for allow for subjectivism. He defines relativism as "making meaning *relative to* a form of life."[58] By this he means that relativism can be defined as meaning in action and context rather than meaning as some fixed standard that is waiting to be discovered. Smith argues that correspondence and representationalist views of language and truth are insufficient to account for human growth and formation and opts instead for a pragmatist understanding.[59] He goes on to defend his view of God's revelation as being authoritative but does so from a pragmatic perspective rather than representationalist perspective. As described earlier, Smith holds Lindbeck in high regard for his development of relativism. However, Frame, commenting on Lindbeck's *The Nature of Doctrine* (and this would land squarely against Smith) says that:

> He has, in effect, presented what is to most of us a new, and in any case interesting, *perspective* on the nature of doctrine which in my view complements, rather than replaces, the other two which he mentions. Doctrine is all three things: propositional truth-claims, expressions of the inner experience of regeneration, and rules for the speech and conduct of God's creatures. No one of these is prior to the others. Lindbeck's book is an excellent

---

58. Smith, *Who's Afraid of Relativism?*, 48.
59. Smith, *Who's Afraid of Relativism?*, 107.

exploration of the third perspective, which is, undoubtedly, the one most neglected in present-day theology.[60]

If Smith looks to Lindbeck as his precursor and inspiration, then one could postulate that Frame would level the same assessment regarding Smith's understanding of encountering God and our transformation as a result of our knowledge of him. In Frame's estimation, Smith's works would be an exploration of the situational perspective, but without a robust exploration of the normative and existential, it falls short of representing the whole picture of CSF.

For Smith, relativism and representationalism seem to be in conflict, but as David Vander Laan points out, this is false dichotomy.[61] While the relativistic account for truth is important and informative, it ultimately fails to account for any notion of a representative understanding of truth.[62] As Theissen goes on to point out, "Communities of practice too can err, a problem that Smith fails to acknowledge."[63] While Smith believes that communities of practice and liturgy are the primary way that we are formed into Christ, these communities of practice and faith must start with being tethered to some truth. Without such a grounding, they can become communities that steep people in whatever relativistic truth commitments they currently understand to be truth. This does not provide people with a reliable, much less Christian, path to CSF.

Triperspectivalism provides a way for us to better understand Smith's proposals without giving into a modernist approach to formation. The concept of doctrine, devotion, and duty as a nexus of formation and discipleship enhances existing models and stands on its own. Triperspectivalism is a potential gold mine of a resource in CSF. For churches and Christians, discipleship does not need to follow a linear pattern of development and growth in godliness. Instead, triperspectivalism offers a holistic and Trinitarian approach to discipleship that could produce more spiritually well-nourished and more epistemically well-resourced formational efforts.

60. Frame, "Review."
61. Laan, "Review," 401–03.
62. Theissen, "Review Article," 174.
63. Theissen, "Review Article," 175.

CHAPTER 6

A Vision of Trinitarian Formation

We arrive at the end of our journey. The vehicle has trodden the path. We have muddied the tires. The gas runs low. All that remains is that we take a look at how our new model weathered the terrain. What was the point of this journey in the first place? The argument that has been developed begins with the reality that modern Evangelical conceptions of discipleship and formation are both unclear and divergent from biblical concepts of formation. A triad of doctrine, devotion, and duty has been put forward from triperspectivalism to suggest a more faithful and helpful philosophy of formation and discipleship. The usefulness of this triad was tested by examining the CSF philosophy of James K. A. Smith. The triad of doctrine, devotion, and duty was able to provide both a way to analyze Smith's philosophy and show deficiencies in his approach.

With the triperspectival approach to formation, we have a durable and theologically robust approach to discipleship. Because of this, it would useful to explore the implications of this new way to think about CSF. Now that we have put both Frame and Smith in conversation, we are better positioned to understand some vulnerabilities and opportunities with each. Smith has developed a philosophy of CSF that insists that desire is to be cultivated by Christian liturgy as the primary formational method. Frame's triperspectivalism as represented by the triad of doctrine, devotion, and duty provides an integrated approach to CSF that offsets some of the liabilities inherent in modernist approaches to discipleship that result in linear schemes of formation.

THE IMPORTANCE OF DESIRE/AFFECTIONS OR THE EXISTENTIAL PERSPECTIVE IN FORMATION

Desire, affections, and love have a long history of significant emphasis in CSF. This has been demonstrated from the hearts of the Israelites in the Bible (Ezek 14:5), to Jesus's teaching about the central importance of the heart (Matt 15:18–20), to the fourth and fifth centuries with Augustine discussing the will and affections.[1] Jonathan Edwards was not the first but has been one of the most vocal and famous Reformed Evangelical proponents of the importance of affections in CSF. Affections for Edwards cannot be faked. They are a grace that God gives and must be nurtured. By affections, Edwards meant the part of the will (and desire) that was directed at loving God and doing what God wants. Edwards listed out twelve proofs of godly affections.[2] The point is that affections have long been a fundamental concern for God's people. James K. A. Smith builds upon this tradition and provides further development from a liturgical and phenomenological framework.

For Smith, "You are what you love because you live toward what you *want*."[3] An approach to formation that is only focused on worldview

> is an approach that unwittingly overestimates the influence of thinking and conscious deliberation and thus tends to overlook and underestimate the power and force of all kinds of unconscious or subconscious processes that orient our being-in-the-world.[4]

1. Augustine, *Confessions.*
2. Edwards, *Religious Affections*, 96.
3. Smith, *You Are What You Love*, 13.
4. Smith, *You Are What You Love*, 13.

Instead of a traditional modernist approach to formation through an encounter with the truth at a cognitive and evidentialist level, Smith flips the script and argues that formation must begin with desire and affection. Modernism typically treats concepts as linear and black and white. The irony here is that in attempting to combat modernistic approaches to formation and virtue, he seems simply to reuse modernistic arguments to prove his point, that formation is linear instead of holistic, something the triperspectival approach provides in full.

Triperspectivalism honors the importance of affections and desire in CSF by placing them appropriately in context. Using the triadic focal point of devotion, the importance of desire and affection is maintained as an essential existential perspective of knowledge. Desire and affections, including our inner world of emotions, are an indispensable aspect of CSF. The opportunity with triperspectivalism is to avoid false formulations wherein Christians are led to believe that circumstances, affections, or beliefs are the primary entry point to formation. As Eric Johnson points out, formation—or therapy, in his emphasis—"seek[s] to repair the split as much as is possible in this age."[5]

THE ROLE OF SCRIPTURE IN FORMATION

One consideration which deserves further scrutiny is the proper place of Scripture in the process of formation. It is important to clearly explore and examine whether Smith's claims do in fact denigrate and undermine the authority of Scripture. Smith's arguments for the primacy of desire in CSF borders on an abandonment of the normative nature of Scripture, or at least seems to logically result in this. The norming norm of Scripture becomes a tool for the community of faith in liturgy rather than the authoritative guide for the community of faith. Rather than the Word of God shaping the community, the community shapes the Word of God. This is not to say that different communities of faith will not take different positions

5. Johnson, *God and Soul Care*, 196.

on Scripture, but that Scripture should serve as the covenant document of the community of faith.

"Smith does not appear to take into account the reciprocal dynamics operative in ritualized processes."[6] In other words, the intellect and body shape one another. Instead of Smith acknowledging that the normative, existential, and situational all interact and inform one another, he creates a false dichotomy between the intellectual enterprise of worldview formation and the more subjective, inward gut-level affections of people that are shaped by liturgy. Liturgy for Smith, is "a certain species of ritual practice that [aims] to do nothing less than shape our identity by shaping our desire for what we envision as the kingdom—the idea of human flourishing."[7] It is liturgy that Smith believes to be the most important in CSF. Liturgy is the entry point to formation. This is what shapes desire, which in turn shapes belief. This proposition has major implications for the authority of Scripture in the lives of Christians. If the intellect and "norming norm" of Scripture finds its authoritative home downstream of both liturgy and desire, then it would seem that the authority of Scripture itself could become easily undermined.

It is also important to note the potential vulnerability of triperspectivalism with regard to the priority of Scripture. Because triperspectivalism validates multiple perspectives, it could be misconstrued to place Scripture as equivalent to affections or situations. Responding to this potential weakness of triperspectivalism, Timothy Miller proposes that the normative should set "the boundaries for the other perspectives" reflecting the order within the Trinity.[8] In this sense, Miller proposes a "processional triperspectivalism" in which the normative mirrors the authority of God the Father in being the first among equals. However, equating Scripture with the normative perspective is not exactly how Frame would describe it. Scripture stands outside of the three perspectives, so to speak, and we approach Scripture from the three perspectives.

6. Turley, "Practicing the Kingdom," 138.

7. Smith, *Desiring the Kingdom*, 87.

8. Tim Miller in email to the author, April 18, 2019.

Scripture must be regarded as the covenant document with which God reveals himself to his people. We experience God through Bible reading in a triadic fashion. We approach the Bible from the normative (doctrinal), existential (devotional), and situational (dutiful) perspectives so that our engagement with the Bible is holistic. This keeps us from rigid fundamentalism and unhinged liberalism. Instead, we come to the Bible acknowledging our creatureliness and contingency.

CSF THROUGH A TRIPERSPECTIVALISM LENS

If CSF consists of approaches to spirituality that are distinctly rooted in the Christian faith and seek to form our material and immaterial capacities in their ability to connect with God and glorify him in life, then triperspectivalism can be utilized to supplement the goals of the enterprise. As stated earlier, a recapitulation of this definition using triperspectivalism would be that CSF seeks to form our *duty, doctrine, and devotion.* To further simplify this approach while honoring it's theological and philosophical foundation, we can refer to it as Trinitarian formation Let's explore some protentional upsides of using this triad in CSF or discipleship.

Trinitarian formation provides CSF with a grid for engaging the capacities of people. David Clark, while not commenting directly on triperspectivalism, makes an observation which corresponds with Trinitarian formation and CSF; "In order to support Christian living, theology provides true, orthodox interpretation (What is life like?), direction (What should I do?), and encouragement (Why should I do it?)."[9] This sounds very much like a Framean triad. Theology itself provides a vision for life that is triperspectival in orientation. This shows that theology is a formational experience.

While CSF at its best should focus on the renewal and restoration of people, it can focus too exclusively on a singular capacity for renewal. This can lead to an unbalanced obsession with one perspective typically to the detriment of other perspectives. Think of how many Christians suffer from spiritual navel gazing, constantly

9. Clark, *To Know and Love God,* 232.

looking for impurities in their own lives in terms of motives. When the affections become the sole focus of formation and development, the mind and actions typically suffer. People become paralyzed in decision making and moving forward because they are so intent on verifying that their affections and intentions for every decision are pure and holy. Foolishness and inaction result from this decision paralysis. Wisdom is developed in our minds by having the ability to be discerning and make the best decisions we can given our limitations in life. However, in spiritual paralysis, wisdom is not developed because instead of learning from lived experience, Christians get stuck trying to perfect our motives and desires before acting. Inaction leads to further lack of development because the paralysis to decide has left the situational perspective dependent on the affective. Theological learning is placed below affections and many Christians become paralyzed without sensing a large certainty that they are operating from pure motives.

Trinitarian formation provides a helpful antidote to this by offering a balanced approach to formation. In a Trinitarian model of discipleship, we acknowledge our limitations and creaturehood knowing that we will never achieve pure motives. Of course, we should be self-reflective, but we don't wait around until we achieve purity. We move forward in confidence trusting the grace of God. We grow as we go.

Unfortunately, CSF can also focus too much on our standing in salvation rather than a renewal of capacities. This can be seen in CSF that focuses on threats rather than assurance of salvation. Rather than growth in knowing God being rooted in his love for us, some theories of CSF promote a version of CSF and discipleship that fosters a suspicious spirit towards oneself and others regarding our salvific standing.

However, the grounding of our growth is the grace of God and the judgment of God poured out on Jesus. With Trinitarian formation, one can readily engage the capacities of people for renewal. For example, the intellect, when thought of through the lens of the normative perspective, can be engaged in CSF. The intellect can be renewed and cultivated in such a way as to honor God. All the while, we are able to acknowledge that even our intellectual development is not holy and is easily influenced by outside sources. Development of the intellect can come through Scripture memory, counseling, Christian education, etc. The affections and will of people can be renewed to make godly choices and have godly affections. This is the opportunity that Smith provides in his proposition that liturgy is the way to the gut. With Trinitarian formation, the actions of people and their situation in life can be engaged with CSF practices from the situational perspective. This highlights the formational nature of liturgy. From this perspective, one can be renewed in their life by stopping certain sin patterns before they start, going on walks, maintaining a healthy diet, finding new friends, creating healthy relational boundaries, serving within a church, etc. All of this can be done with a focus on the renewal of capacities rather than obsessive concern with God loving me more if I obey (a false notion in itself because God's love for you and me is only conditioned on the obedience and righteousness of Christ imputed to us).

Using Trinitarian formation, we will engage a common issue plaguing many people today, the use of pornography. From a Christian perspective, the use of pornography is not good (Matt 5:28) and not what God desires for people. However, if Christians find themselves entangled in a pattern of using pornography, what are they to do?

For some people, they believe that it is enough to tell the Christian to stop and remove the means of viewing pornography (situational perspective). This can be done through internet filters or by removing the internet altogether. Once the means to access is removed, the problem will go away. If you cannot access a bad thing, you won't consume a bad thing. Then by refraining from the use of pornography, you will be more mature.

For others, the problem is intellectual. The person viewing pornography has been believing lies and have not filled their mind with the Word of God (normative perspective). Therefore, the prescription is more Bible memory.[10] Once you know enough about the Bible or think about the Bible enough or remember verses about the pleasures of God, you will no longer look at pornography,

10. For example, nouthetic counseling believes that Scripture is sufficient for any true Christian to overcome patterns of sin.

or so the thinking goes. You must dwell on the Word of God as the primary strategy to combat this sin. And the Bible testifies to the importance of setting our mind on God's word and reflecting on things above (Col 3:2).

Yet others insist that the main issue is one of affections (existential perspective). People who use pornography have misshapen desires and therefore make bad decisions in choosing to use pornography.[11] They have heart idols that they have not discovered through Christian versions of cognitive behavioral therapy. The remedy to this would be either to become a Christian or ask God to change one's desires. This could be done by cultivating desires for godly things through Bible reading, meditating on spiritual truths, participating in godly liturgy. This can be seen in some Christian circles that promote idol-hunting (searching one's heart idols) as a primary means of formation. The idea would be that if you are able to identify your idol, then you can repent of the idol. Once you repent of the idol and understand more clearly why you do what you do, the sin behavior should stop.

In Trinitarian formation, we can see that no one method is perfect. In fact, the over-reliance on one perspective for the renewal of people could be detrimental to their spiritual health. All three perspectives are essential in forming people and different people may initially find one perspective more helpful than others. Believing that Bible memory is the only method which renews people in such a way that they no longer participate in the use of pornography is misleading and self-deceptive for example. Or, consider the idea that once one knows the reasons (idols) that are driving their use of pornography then that (the realization of and repentance from idols) will reduce their participation in it. While knowing what is below the surface or driving one's behavior is key to transformation, it is by no means a one-size-fits-all approach. Just ask anyone struggling with pornographic use how many times they have tried to repent of their heart idols in order to get better and how that has left them.

11. Cusick, *Surfing for God.*

Trinitarian formation can provide CSF with a balance lacking in many CSF philosophies. Not only that, but it can be used as a tool of analysis for other theories of CSF. This is closely related to the argument presented above in describing attempts to combat the use of pornography. Many forms of CSF can overly rely on one or even two aspects of triperspectivalism while neglecting the others. Using triperspectivalism to analyze the usefulness and validity of philosophies of CSF will prevent certain practices from being over-ly prescribed. For example, Trinitarian formation could be used in a denomination to assess its approach to and understanding of discipleship. Southern Baptist discipleship strategies could be ana-lyzed using this approach in order to enhance their own approach. Balance is important in CSF because as humans we are hardwired to look for salvation in a means or method that we utilize rather than Christ.

A balanced approach to CSF based on triperspectivalism will cultivate and maintain a posture of grace and humility amongst people. Many people in churches suffer under the expectation that the renewal of their capacities will only come from one of the three perspectives. Churches and movements can preach that spiritual vitality as expressed emotionally is the ultimate measure of spiritual maturity. For example, many charismatic movements lead people to believe that the affections and individual experience of either the presence of God or certain gifts are a barometer for one's spiritual health. These movements create disciples that either despair of their lack of personal experience or hold the expectation of experience as a trump card of assessment against other churches and Christians. Triperspectivalism would push against this exclusivistic approach to Christian wholeness.

Alternatively, churches can preach that behavior modification and correction is the gold standard for spiritual maturity (situ-ational). We must behave in step with the gospel to grow (which is true, but only partly true). Churches with this view of formation tend to assess maturity in the situational perspective by analyzing one's ability to obey the rules. Yet other churches and para-church ministries could say that more knowledge and Bible memory is the means to maturity and renewal (normative). If you want to progress as a Christian, you must take classes and read books to mature as a person (once again true, but only partly true). Triperspectivalism promotes a balance that challenges the exclusivity of each of these claims.

This balance is articulated well by Esther Lightcap Meek when she says,

> Philosophers and ordinary people have sometimes associated knowledge with one of these sectors in a way that has blinded them to the others. They might say that knowledge just has to do with "the way things are," overlooking what I bring to it and how I tell. Other people have overdone the "what I bring to it," to the exclusion of what is there. Still others have thought knowledge was just about the text, or the Scriptures, leading them to overlook and discredit the world and body that even in their own efforts they couldn't not help but rely on. Capable and effective knowing require intentional (not necessarily explicit) employment of all three dimensions.[12]

Meek articulates well the opportunity for balance which triperspectivalism can offer in CSF.

Additionally, Trinitarian formation can provide a CSF grid that honors the tension inherent in theological anthropology. Theological anthropology deals with the issues of human composition and the image of God. With regard to human composition, a triperspectival approach to CSF is useful because it honors the tension between the material and immaterial. Whichever way one defines the dichotomous nature of human composition as biblically represented, a triperspectival CSF approach honors the reality that people are embodied and yet immaterial.

We exist within a particular time and place with a particular people. There is only so much that one can do to escape this context. We are formed relationally before we are even aware we are being formed. From a situational perspective, the embodied nature of people is honored by thinking relationally about our story and context. It also recognizes that our bodies shape our souls in some

---

12. Meek, *Loving to Know*, 82–83.

ways. From an existential and normative perspective, the reality that we are also immaterial is maintained and honored as Trinitarian formation addresses affections and knowledge. The mind-body problem is not a problem in Trinitarian formation. Instead of the soul and body becoming a dichotomy in CSF, it provides a balance.

Consider the current tumult in American society over issues of race and justice, and how triperspectivalism might provide a way forward. The conversation over race and justice within the American church has historically been poor. This has been a failure of the American church, and it tarnishes the witness of the church to a watching world. Churches should rightly concern themselves with issues of justice in society such as abortion or race-based discrimination. God intends for his people to be a city on a hill. We are to be known for our love for others. Instead, we seem to be known for our inability to even talk honestly about issues of race and justice. The opportunity before us with triperspectivalism is to change the way these conversations can be held.

In some streams of philosophical thought, lived experience based in standpoint epistemology is the penultimate means to knowledge. Lived experience is thought to be the unique experience of those who have experienced oppression which produces knowledge which cannot be otherwise acquired. For many crying out for justice today, this lived experience is the primary means of knowledge. For them, denying their lived experience is akin to denying that any injustice took place at all. However, others approach issues of race and justice from a fact-based analysis of reality. They are most concerned with the data and statistics related to injustice. These datum and stats become explainers and at times minimize the real experiences some have had regarding racism in America. For them, cries of injustice based in lived experience come across as disproportionate at best and intentionally dishonest or manipulative at worst.

Instead, triperspectivalism honors facts, experience, and feelings. The lived experience, when understood in terms of triperspectivalism, can in part be correlative with the existential perspective. There are countless stories of individuals from minority ethnicities, particularly blacks, historically experiencing discrimination at the hands of law-enforcement officers or other systems of power. Not only this, but there is a history of systemic racial injustice in America which has created suspicion from the black community. However, the existential is neither primary nor exclusive in terms of knowledge. It is one part of three.

Similarly, the data and facts regarding discrimination and police encounters is also important. The wide disparity between the total amount of blacks killed in shootings other than police encounters and those particularly killed at the hands of police officers is not insignificant. It is particular knowledge, but it is simply one part of the whole. Most of the polarization around race and justice occurs because these two camps view themselves as opposites. Instead, with triperspectivalism, we have a model which breaks a binary lock that only entrenches polarities. We can honor the embodied experience of blacks in America and take into account their feelings and perceptions while also honoring and paying attention to the facts and data. More than that, we can look to the norming norm of Scripture to teach us the standards of God's world in which all people are made in the image of the Son of God. Churches concerned with justice would be wise to embrace a model such as triperspectivalism rather than worldly movements or philosophies which offer no redemption (such as Critical Race Theory).

The church should be the model of listening well and speaking the truth. Instead, we have resorted to tribal talking points resembling the culture around us. We need to reframe the conversation itself. With triperspectivalism, we have a tool that is formative and constructive for dialogue over issues of race and justice. We need discussion, not division, when we talk about these issues in America. The binary choice to which we sense pressure to conform must be rejected as not only insufficient but also symptomatic of the problem itself, reinforcing tribalism and relational disconnect as a result of sin. Until a tool such as triperspectivalism is utilized, the people in our churches and Christian institutions will flounder and flirt with secular ideologies, whether they be of nationalistic or ethno-centric origin.

Finally, Trinitarian formation allows for different perspectives to be applied at different times depending on what is most helpful. Triperspectivalism admits that all of our knowledge is partial and therefore lends itself to the utilization of self-discovery and curiosity. For example, in Trinitarian formation, one can easily incorporate tools such as personality inventories into a regular diet of prayer and Bible reading in order to better understand one's proclivities. Rather than limiting and thwarting self-discovery as some discipleship models can promote by equating discipleship with taking a class, Trinitarian formation encourages a humility of oneself that promotes curiosity about oneself, others, and God.

John Frame believes triperspectivalism is useful in the journey of the Christian life:

> In its normative perspective, [we work on] obeying God's commands. In the situational perspective, we apply those commands to each situation we encounter. And in the existential perspective, we, through the Spirit, seek to be transformed. (Rom 12:2)[13]

Triperspectivalism is not just for philosophers and theologians, it is for all people who want to know God. Anyone seeking to know God more and grow in godliness can benefit from triperspectivalism.

---

13. Frame, *Theology in Three Dimensions*, 75.

CHAPTER 7

Ministries in Light of Trinitarian Formation

THE END OF THIS road is only the beginning of new ones. My aim has been to show that triperspectivalism as a theological method is much more than a theological method. It is a tool that can be employed in making disciples. We have only test driven the method in this book so that we could prove its durability. In closing, my hope is to stimulate your vision of how this model could be useful.

Triperspectivalism as a pedagogical tool is a stout and practical theological method that has wide ranging implications in the field of CSF. By utilizing Trinitarian formation, churches can advance helpful and holistic ministries with respect to CSF and discipleship. There is great value in the potential implementation of a triperspectival philosophy of CSF by gospel-centered churches and ministries. By adopting the approach of Trinitarian formation, churches would be pulling from a rich history of Trinitarian thought in making disciples. This Trinitarian foundation could prove impactful in creating a disciple-making culture that is less grounded in pragmatism and more in Christian theological tradition.

If triperspectivalism is used as a lens for analyzing other CSF practices and philosophies, then it can also easily be used as a tool to assess the implementation of theologies of sanctification and discipleship. Consider sanctification. Grudem defines sanctification as "*a progressive work of God and man that makes us more and more free from sin and like Christ in our actual lives.*"[1] While Grudem's definition unnecessarily excludes the reality of positional sanctification as seen in Paul's letters, he does posit some ways in which people can grow more like Christ and in what capacities. Grudem proposes that sanctification engages our intellect, emotions, our will, our spirit, and our physical bodies.[2] These summaries of the engagement of sanctification are unnecessarily complicated and anthropologically confusing. While Grudem's five categories are biblically faithful in general, could we not also be biblically faithful using a triperspectival lens? For example, as Smith has stated and Frame has alluded to, what if we simply helped people think of our capacities in terms of head, heart, and hands?

With regard to discipleship, triperspectivalism can be utilized to assess the balance and goals of discipleship. Much like a tire that requires balancing when first placed on a wheel, so too should discipleship not only be biblically based but also well balanced.[3] Discipleship within Evangelicalism in general is the result of an outworking of the theology of sanctification assumed. If one assumes that sanctification is progressive, then discipleship in practice becomes a means to further that sanctification.[4] Discipleship is widely defined as following Jesus more and learning to walk in his ways. In Trinitarian formation, one does not fall into the trap of making behavior or affections or knowledge the priority. Triperspectivalism helps maintain both a distinction and balance in discipleship. It emphasizes all three ways of knowing as legitimate means to experience more of God and grow in Christlikeness.

Further exploration could be possible in studying the correlation of spiritual formation and discipleship through a triadic lens. Michael Wilkins makes use of "three marks of discipleship that Jesus said were evidence of whether a person had truly believed,

---

1. Grudem, *Systematic Theology*, 747. Italics original.

2. Grudem, *Systematic Theology*, 756–57.

3. Wilkins, *Following the Master*, 355.

4. Wilkins, *Following the Master*, 343.

had truly become a disciple."[5] He goes on to correlate the three marks, "abiding in Jesus' word, loving the brethren, and bearing fruit," with three common domains of spiritual disciplines in the history of the church.[6] Further analysis could be provided to discover if there is a correspondence between these three marks and triperspectivalism. For example, abiding in Jesus's word could be considered the normative perspective, loving the brethren the affective, and bearing fruit the situational. Trinitarian formation seems to have been hinted at through church history. Work could be done to analyze other theologians to discover correlations with Trinitarian formation.

With regard to ecclesiology, Trinitarian formation has wide ranging implications. First, if triperspectivalism is a legitimate means of developing CSF practices then the church as a whole would be shaped in its practices. While the very nature and purpose of the church may not change, the practices itself would surely change. The church would be a place where the normative, existential, and situational aspects of our relationship with God and others are cultivated and nurtured. The church would promote and celebrate intellectual transformation, affectional awareness and development, and liturgical and missional engagement. A church saturated with a theology of Trinitarian formation would not be relegated to one aspect of the triad but instead embrace a holistic approach. Every ministry within the church would take on a triperspectival bent. For example, a church that has a men's ministry would be concerned with developing men in their duty, doctrine, and devotional encounter with God and others. It would show the appropriate biblical responsibilities for men in general and provide more specificity with regard to particular relational contexts (duty). The church would show right belief through the Bible and also through practical wisdom (doctrine). A triperspectival men's ministry would also discuss desire, affections, and emotions (existential). All of this would be centered on the gospel so that none of

5. Wilkins, *Following the Master*, 134.
6. Wilkins, *Following the Master*, 134–35.

the perspectives would impinge on the identity of people and their union with Christ.

Second, the church would have a balanced approach to ministry so that none of the perspectives holds a primary place over and against the others. A common paradigm that some churches use is that of the church being a community, cause, and corporation. This common paradigm is easily complemented by a triperspectival approach to CSF where the corporation is the normative, the community is the existential, and the cause is the outward-facing situational.

Think of how a church shaped by triperspectivalism would operate. In the normative perspective where cognitive development is prized, churches would focus on developing the life of the mind. A church concerned with the life of the mind would not settle for resources that are weak minded. Many Evangelical churches settle for resources and teachings that are designed to reach the most people. Discipleship and formation resources are chosen and implemented based on what is selling and is most popular. Instead, a church that took seriously the life of the mind would utilize resources that were not just most popular but are most stimulating intellectually.

This is why at my church we recommend that church members borrow or buy commentaries written by scholars to deepen their understanding of the Bible. A discipleship group that has been trained in head, heart, hands, at our church recently used an academic commentary to supplement its Bible study.[7] We do not hesitate to recommend resources that are more academic in nature. Christians of all people should be people who value rigorous and clear thinking. We worship the God of all language and thought. He made everything. Settling for a version of Christianity in which the cognitive aspects of formation are reduced to the value of whatever is most popular and easiest to understand only perpetuates an Evangelical subculture that is anti-intellectual. This cognitive appreciation and engagement would not just be for the sake of knowing more, but it would be for the sake of holiness and

---

7. Bailey, *Paul through Mediterranean Eyes*.

transformation. It would also not be held as the primary way of knowing but in tension with the other perspectives.

Think of a church that believed a core aspect of knowing was affective or emotive knowing. Churches typically land in two extremes when it comes to emotional expression. On the one hand I have been to churches with the "frozen chosen" who simply stand and sit with very little emotive expression. On the other hand, I have been to churches that champion the emotive to such a degree that to not emote is to not experience God. If one does not express oneself emotionally, one's relationship with God, or at least the vibrancy of that relationship, is called into question. Both are extremes and a church that values affections, desires, and emotions from a triperspectival understanding would be a place where both extremes could come together. A church that valued the importance of affections and desires in formation would help create a culture of authenticity where people could share what it is they most desire. Many Christians seem to wear a mask over their desires so as to make them more acceptable to others. A church that took seriously desire would not settle for a masked version of desire. They would encourage people to be honest before God and others while ensuring a culture of relational safety was strong in order to receive the honesty of people.

A church rich in Trinitarian formation would dive into formational tools like emotional intelligence. Church members would be encouraged to practice spiritual disciplines that bring to light the false and true self. A church that took seriously the affections of their people would create a climate in which emotions were not seen as dirty or inconvenient but instead ways of knowing which are implicit. Taking one's past trauma or pain to God in Christ Jesus would be a keystone habit in the formation of people at this church as people are encouraged to be emotionally vulnerable and have Jesus redeem their story.

Imagine a church which championed the perspective of the situational. Many American churches are activistic in orientation due to the history of Evangelicalism in America as a revivalist movement. This leads more liberally minded churches to engage in social justice and acts of mercy. It also leads more conservatively minded churches to engage in evangelism and conversionism. Not only this, but many churches can focus specifically on behavior modification as the standard of formation. However, in a church that held the situational in tension with the other perspectives, the outworking of the Christian life in the world would just be one more means of knowing and growing. Behavior in this church would simply be a way that we can begin to know God. Rather than wait until everyone has their doctrine in order to be able to lead or serve in the church, this church would recognize that sometimes the first step in growth is obedience and action. Behavior modification at this church would be minimized because behaviors, sinful or otherwise, would just be one means of knowing oneself and God. Sinful behaviors would be explored through the cognitive (false beliefs) and affective (sinful desires) lens of the individual. Meaning that sometimes sinful behavior would be an indicator like an engine overheating indicator on a dashboard. Rather than just turning off the sensor, we should investigate the problem further.

There are major implications of triperspectivalism in CSF from the situational perspective. Because context develops and changes over time, the situational outworkings of God's truth are constantly in need of being re-examined. While God's word does not change, the application of God's word will look different over time. Trinitarian formation can serve as a useful grid to develop situational applications of God's word in a manner consistent with God's ways. The way we pursue the outworking of God's will in our lives individually and corporately requires a theological method that is sensitive to our creaturehood and embodied state. Triperspectivalism embraces that reality. Rather than wringing the Bible into some kind of fortune book for decision making, the Bible is held as the norming norm that informs and interacts with the other two perspectives. Think of how one would chose a vocation or career. Many Christians are led to the conclusion that they should read the Bible and discern from the Bible which particular career is right for them. This is possible. However, reading the Bible triperspectivally takes into account how we read it, from what culture, and it also takes into account our desires. Trinitarian formation allows the room for exploration and experimentation of giftings and calling rather than waiting for a sign from God to take action.

Consideration is also needed to explore the relationship of triperspectivalism and the lingering effects of sin in people. Because Trinitarian formation disciples people in their head, heart, and hands, it is important to understand how the lingering effects of the fall impede these efforts. One could speculate regarding the noetic effects of the fall with respect to the life of the mind. Or one could consider psychological and emotional vulnerabilities in the realm of the affective. Not to mention, an analysis of desire and the sinfulness of particular desires could be explored. As an example, currently within Evangelicalism, there is a debate regarding the sinfulness of homosexual desire. The question is framed in this way: Can one remain celibate while honoring their homosexual desire (as opposed to squelching or suppressing said desire) and be considered faithfully walking with Christ? Within the scope of Trinitarian formation, this is a legitimate question to be raised and explored.

Furthermore, biblical studies could be conducted tracing a Trinitarian formation from creation through fall, redemption, and restoration. A biblical theology of Trinitarian formation could be developed in this way. It could be that in the biblical narrative there are hints at the formational triad established by God for connection with him. Not only this, there could be a triperspectival correspondence between the temptation and sin in the garden (Gen 3:16), the three temptations of Christ (Matt 4:1–11), and the warnings of John about the love of the world (1 John 2:16). Consider how Eve was tempted to doubt what God said (normative), she was tempted in her desire (existential), and tempted to act out of step with what God commanded (situational). This temptation and fall into sin was similarly combatted by Christ in his temptations. Each episode deals with three concepts under the main concept of sin. In this way, a triad for sin could possibly be constructed that would then provide clarity on how sin impedes efforts at CSF. Not only this but one could look to Revelation and see hints of what it might look like to glorify God in eternity in a triadic fashion.

Deeper work from Trinitarian formation could be conducted to explore the feasibility of measuring the progression of spiritual maturity in each of the three perspectives (or how this endeavor is connected to a theology of sanctification). Tools for pastors and church leaders could be established to serve as intake forms for processing the most applicable manner in which to care for people head, heart, or hands.[8] While purely objective measurements would not be possible, markers or indicators of maturity in each perspective could be suggested and scrutinized in a real-world setting. A ministry research project could consist of developing a triperspectival CSF methodology for a church and then assessing if people grew in spiritual maturity through metrics developed in the project.

Triperspectivalism is a useful, biblically faithful, and intellectually satisfying theological method that, when employed as Trinitarian formation, reaps a bounty of growth in our connection with God. Seeing formation in terms of duty, doctrine, and devotion maintains a balanced, creaturely, and biblical faithful model for knowing God. Without Trinitarian formation, churches and other disciple making ministries will risk creating malformed and malnourished disciples. This is both inevitable and unnecessary. Our God is triune. The opportunity before us is to ground our discipleship in that reality. Otherwise, people will be left creating modernist schemes of development which dehumanize people. Christians suffer under the weight of enormous pressure to measure up in this world. Our God beckons us to come and find rest. Trinitarian formation is an essential way to help people know the rest which God offers them. In our mission to make disciples of all nations, Trinitarian formation is an indispensable tool with which to fulfill that task.

---

8. Denver Seminary makes use of a similar model in its training and mentoring program.

Bibliography

Anderson, James N. "Presuppositionalism and Frame's Epistemology." In *Speaking the Truth in Love: The Theology of John M. Frame,* edited by John J. Hughes, 431–59. Phillipsburg, NJ: Presbyterian and Reformed, 2009.

Anderson, Tawa J. "Imagining the Kingdom: How Worship Works." *Christian Scholars Review* 43, no. 2 (Winter 2014) 187–91.

Augustine of Hippo. *Confessions.* Translated by Henry Chadwick. Oxford: Oxford University Press, 2008.

Bailey, Kenneth E. *Paul through Mediterranean Eyes.* Downers Grove, IL: InverVarsity, 2011.

Barna Group. *The State of Discipleship: A Barna Report Produced in Partnership with The Navigators.* Ventura, CA: Barna, 2015.

Belcher, Jodi L. A. "Imaging the Kingdom: How Worship Works." *Anglican Theological Review* 96, no. 4 (Fall 2014) 792–93.

Blomberg, Doug. "'The Heart Has Reasons That Reason Cannot Know': Thinking, Feeling, and Willing in Learning." *Journal of Education and Christian Belief* 17, no. 1 (2013) 61–77.

Boa, Kenneth. *Conformed to His Image: Biblical and Practical Approaches to Spiritual Formation.* Grand Rapids: Zondervan, 2001.

Calvin, John. *Institutes of the Christian Religion.* Translated by Ford Lewis Battles. Edited by John T. McNeill. Louisville, KY: Westminster John Knox, 2011.

Clark, David K. *To Know and Love God: Foundations of Evangelical Theology.* Edited by John S. Feinberg. Wheaton, IL: Crossway, 2003.

Cusick, Michael John. *Surfing for God: Discovering the Divine Desire Beneath the Sexual Struggle.* Nashville: Thomas Nelson, 2012.

Edwards, Jonathan. *Religious Affections.* Vol. 2, *The Works of Jonathan Edwards.* Edited by John E. Smith. New Haven, CT: Yale University Press, 2009.

Erickson, Millard J. *Christian Theology.* 3rd ed. Grand Rapids: Baker Academic, 2013.

Estep, James R., and Jonathan H. Kim, eds. *Christian Formation: Integrating Theology and Human Development.* Nashville: Broadman & Holman, 2010.

Faroe, Charles E. "In Pursuit of a Holistic Christian Pedagogy: Affectivity in James K. A. Smith's *Desiring the Kingdom.*" *Journal of European Baptist Studies* 13, no. 3 (May 2013) 12–23.

Fourth, Michael. "Christian Reflections on the Phenomenological Epistemology of Maurice Merleau-Ponty." *IIIM Magazine Online* 5, no. 22 (June 2003) 1–20.

Frame, John M. *Doctrine of the Christian Life.* Phillipsburg, NJ: Presbyterian and Reformed, 2008.

———. *Doctrine of the Knowledge of God.* Vol. 1, *A Theology of Lordship.* Phillipsburg, NJ: Presbyterian and Reformed, 1987.

———. *A History of Western Philosophy and Theology.* Phillipsburg, NJ: Presbyterian and Reformed, 2015.

———. "A Primer on Perspectivalism." *The Works of John Frame & Vern Poythress.* Last modified May 14, 2008. https://frame-poythress.org/a-primer-on-perspectivalism-revised-2008/.

———. "Review of Lindbeck's *The Nature of Doctrine.*" *The Works of John Frame & Vern Poythress.* May 25, 2012. https://frame-poythress.org/review-of-lindbecks-the-nature-of-doctrine/.

———. *Systematic Theology: An Introduction to Christian Belief.* Phillipsburg, NJ: Presbyterian and Reformed, 2013.

———. *Theology in Three Dimensions: A Guide to Triperspectivalism and Its Significance.* Phillipsburg, NJ: Presbyterian and Reformed, 2017.

Groothuis, Douglas. "The Postmodernist Challenge to Theology." *Themelios* 25, no. 1 (1999) 4–22.

Grudem, Wayne. *Systematic Theology: An Introduction to Biblical Doctrine.* Grand Rapids: Zondervan, 2000.

Hibbs, Pierce Taylor. "Do You See How I See? The Trinitarian Roots of Human Perception." *The Westminster Theological Journal* 79, no. 1 (Spring 2017) 59–76.

Hughes, John J., ed. *Speaking the Truth in Love: The Theology of John M. Frame.* Phillipsburg, NJ: Presbyterian and Reformed, 2009.

Johnson, Eric L. *God & Soul Care: The Therapeutic Resources of the Christian Faith.* Downers Grove, IL: InterVarsity, 2017.

Karlberg, Mark W. "On the Theological Correlation of Divine and Human Language: A Review Article." *Journal of Evangelical Theology* 32 (1989) 99–105.

Kilner, John Frederic. *Dignity and Destiny: Humanity in the Image of God.* Grand Rapids: Eerdmans, 2015.

Laan, David Vander. "Review of 'Who's Afraid of Relativism?'" *Christian Scholar's Review* 45, no. 4 (2016) 401–03.

Lindbeck, George. *The Nature of Doctrine: Religion and Theology in a Postliberal Age.* Philadelphia: Westminster, 1984.

Longenecker, Richard N., ed. *Patterns of Discipleship in the New Testament.* Grand Rapids: Eerdmans, 1996.

Macmurray, John. *The Self As Agent.* Atlantic Highlands, NJ: Humanities, 1978.

Bibliography

Maddix, Mark A. "Spiritual Formation and Christian Formation." In *Christian Formation: Integrating Theology and Human Development*, edited by James R. Estep and Jonathan H. Kim, 237–72. Nashville: Broadman & Holman, 2010.

Meek, Esther Lightcap. *Loving to Know: Introducing Covenant Epistemology*. Eugene, OR: Cascade, 2011.

Miller, Timothy E. "The Theological Method of John Frame and Vern Poytress." PhD diss., Westminster Theological Seminary, 2015.

———. *The Triune God of Unity in Diversity: An Analysis of Perspectivalism, the Trinitarian Theological Method of John Frame and Vern Poythress*. Phillipsburg, NJ: Presbyterian and Reformed, 2017.

Mohler, Albert. "Part II: To be cool or to be a church? A secular culture forces churches to choose when it comes to biblical sexuality." February 15, 2019. *The Briefing Podcast*. Podcast audio, 27:27. https://albertmohler.com/2019/02/15/briefing-2-15-19.

Moreland, J. P. "Spiritual Formation and the Nature of the Soul." *Christian Education Journal* 4, no. 2 (2000) 25–43.

Morlan, David S. "A Review on James K. A. Smith's 'Cultural Liturgies' Series." *Bulletin of Ecclesial Theology* 3, no. 1 (June 2016) 1–13.

Nichols, Bridget. "James K. A. Smith, *Imagining the Kingdom*: How Worship Works." *Theology* 117, no. 6 (Nov–Dec 2014) 447–48.

Noble, T. A. *Holy Trinity: Holy People*. Eugene, OR: Cascade, 2013.

Parrett, Gary A., and Steve Kang. *Teaching the Faith, Forming the Faithful: A Biblical Vision for Education in the Church*. Downers Grove, IL: InterVarsity, 2009.

Payne, Don J. *Already Sanctified: A Theology of the Christian Life in Light of God's Completed Work*. Grand Rapids: Baker Academic, 2020.

Penner, Myron B. "Cartesian Anxiety, Perspectivalism, and Truth: A Response to J. P. Moreland." *Philosophia Christi* 8, no. 1 (2006) 85–98.

Peterson, Eugene. *A Long Obedience in the Same Direction: Discipleship in an Instant Society*. Downers Grove, IL: InterVarsity, 2000.

Petersen, William H. "*Desiring the Kingdom*: Worship, Worldview, and Cultural Formation." *Anglican Theological Review* 94, no. 4 (Fall 2012) 772–75.

———. "Imagining the Kingdom: How Worship Works." *Anglican Theological Review* 97, no. 4 (Fall 2015) 732–34.

Pickett, Todd E. "You Are What You Love: The Spiritual Power of Habit" *Journal of Spiritual Formation and Soul Care* 9, no. 2 (Fall 2016) 304–07.

Plass, Richard, and James Cofield. *The Relational Soul: Moving from False Self to Deep Connection*. Downers Grove, IL: InterVarsity, 2014.

Powlison, David. "Frame's Ethics: Working the Implications for Pastoral Care." In *Speaking the Truth in Love: The Theology of John M. Frame*, edited by John J. Hughes, 759–77. Phillipsburg, NJ: Presbyterian and Reformed, 2009.

Rolheiser, Ronald. *Against an Infinite Horizon: The Finger of God in Our Everyday Lives*. New York: Crossroad, 2001.

Bibliography

Smets, Duane. "Thinking through Triperspectivalism." *The Resolved Church* (blog). Accessed March, 5, 2019, https://theresolved.com/thinking-through-triper spectivalism.

Smith, James K. A. *Awaiting the King: Reforming Public Theology*. Vol. 3, *Cultural Liturgies*. Grand Rapids: Baker Academic, 2017.

———. *Curriculum Vitae*, Calvin College. Accessed January 4, 2019, https://calvin.edu/contentAsset/raw-data/2d640952-8b99-45b1-bfe5-a66b8121d378/cvresume.

———. *Desiring the Kingdom: Worship Worldview, and Cultural Formation*. Vol. 1, *Cultural Liturgies*. Grand Rapids: Baker Academic, 2009.

———. *Imagining the Kingdom: How Worship Works*. Vol. 2, *Cultural Liturgies*. Grand Rapids: Baker Academic, 2013.

———. "Two Cheers for Worldview: A Response to Elmer John Thiessen." *Journal of Education & Christian Belief* 14, no. 1 (2010) 55–58

———. *Who's Afraid of Relativism? Community, Contingency, and Creaturehood*. Grand Rapids: Baker Academic, 2014.

———. *You Are What You Love: The Spiritual Power of Habit*. Grand Rapids: Brazos, 2016.

Thiessen, Elmer John. "A Review Article of 'Who's Afraid of Relativism?'" *Evangelical Quarterly* 87, no. 2 (2015) 169–75.

———. "Review of 'Educating Our Desires for God's Kingdom.'" *Journal of Education & Christian Belief* 14, no. 1 (2010) 47–53.

Torres, Joseph Emmauel. "Perspectives on Multiperspectivalism." In *Speaking the Truth in Love: The Theology of John M. Frame*, edited by John J. Hughes, 111–36. Phillipsburg, NJ: Presbyterian and Reformed, 2009.

Turley, Stephen Richard. "Practicing the Kingdom: A Critical Appraisal of James K. A. Smith's *Desiring the Kingdom*." *Calvin Theological Journal* 48, no. 1 (April 2013) 131–42.

Van Til, Cornelius. *A Christian Theory of Knowledge*. Nutley, NJ: Presbyterian and Reformed, 1969.

Vanderstelt, Jeff. *Gospel Fluency: Speaking the Truths of Jesus into the Everyday Stuff of Life*. Wheaton, IL: Crossway, 2017.

Vanhoozer, Kevin J. "Worship at the Well: From Dogmatics to Doxology (And Back Again)." *Trinity Journal* 23, no. 1 (2002) 3–16.

Wilkins, Michael J. *Following the Master: A Biblical Theology of Discipleship*. Grand Rapids: Zondervan, 1992.

Willard, Dallas. *The Great Omission: Reclaiming Jesus's Essential Teaching on Discipleship*. New York: HarperOne, 2006.

———. *Renovation of the Heart: Putting on the Character of Christ*. Colorado Springs: NavPress, 2002.

Wittgenstein, Ludwig. *Philosophical Investigation*. 2nd ed. Oxford: Blackwell, 1958.